Black People Can Be So Delusional

by T. Hayden

DORRANCE
PUBLISHING CO
EST. 1920
PITTSBURGH, PENNSYLVANIA 15238

Dorrance Publishing Co
585 Alpha Drive
Pittsburgh, PA 15238
Visit our website at *www.dorrancebookstore.com*

ISBN: 978-1-4809-9141-5
eISBN: 978-1-4809-9399-0

I am going to get right to the point by saying how it really saddens me that so many blacks in this country, mostly low-income, are delusional over extremely important matters in life. These matters include politics and government maneuvers, education, state benefits, preparing for the future, and the incarceration and eradication of blacks. I do not confess to know everything; in fact, what I do know could not even fill up an 8-ounce cup of coffee. I want to warn you; my words are blunt and very direct. Still, I hope all who read this will sit down and take serious stock of their life today, as well as their future tomorrow.

Black People
Can Be So Delusional

POLITICS

I want to jump head first into the realm of politics, a subject on which I do not claim to be an expert. I always watch the presidential campaigns and I always vote. Well, I missed out on voting twice in my life but I made sure to vote for Obama. Although Obama's approval ratings were sometimes low, he did not do any worse than other presidents before him. Truthfully, Obama did a much better job than Bush Jr., who was responsible for putting our country in an even more devastating predicament. Enough said; I want to get to the point of why I chose to speak a little bit about politics.

I will never forget the reaction of black people on the day after Obama was elected in 2008. Through the tears, laughter, and joy of so many, I heard a man say, "We got a black president! Things are gonna change for us now!" I just shook my head. Black people are so delusional. In spite of the historical significance of having the first black president in this country and all the joy that comes with it, I knew that nothing would change for us. Why? Because Barack Obama was the leader of the United States of America, nothing more, nothing less. He did not run this country because he did not possess the power to do so! No president ever has! The wealthiest individuals, the elite 2%, those who own the banks and possess a tremendous amount of power run this country with a tight fist. Don't believe me? Think about the time Obama wanted to pass a law banning certain automatic weapons. After his speech, I said, "Right! Good luck with that one." Did the law pass? Of course not. It never had a chance, not with the wealthiest of the wealthy and the NRA blocking Obama's every move. It was a waste of time for him to have made the effort in the first place, but he had to make himself look good in the eyes of the public. White people love their guns and they are not going to let the government take them away—-no matter how many school shootings or mass murders occur.

Furthermore, Blacks were delusional in thinking they were responsible for getting Obama elected. I am not knocking those who got out and voted; in fact, I'm applauding them. It's just that Blacks make up around 12% of the U.S. population and whites make up roughly 67%. Do the math. It would not have mattered if the entire 12% of Blacks had voted three times. If 67% of Whites had not wanted Obama in office, he never would have made it to the White House. Any time the people who control this country want a particular candidate in office, you had best believe they will do *anything* to make sure it happens.

OBAMA

AND THE WHITE HOUSE

Now, black people, ask yourselves: Did your life get any better while Obama was in office? I didn't think so. In fact, for many black men, life got worse, so bad that it put them six feet in the ground. I am not blaming Obama for this at all. I really believe that white racists cops could not take seeing Obama—-a black man—-in office, so they took it out on other Blacks (Just theorizing). Life got better for many gays; though, and I guess you can say I was a little envious. I have nothing against gays (another minority group) and I mean it. It's just that Obama made sure to help them while he did nothing to help the black race. There are people in the United States who say that *all* people are supposed to help themselves, not look for handouts from the government. This is not what I'm talking about. I'm talking about improving the quality of life for Blacks...in society, employment, and dealing with racist cops. Listen—-because of what Obama did for gays, more of them are getting married and are treated in the same way as heterosexuals. This is all good because I am a firm believer in "doing unto others..." Obama went one-step further by inviting Jason Collins of the NBA to the White House after he *came out of the closet*. How many mothers of murdered black men did Obama invite to the White House? None that I know of. As I remember it, Obama invited individuals, who were a part of the BLACK LIVES MATTER movement, to the White House *after* Micah Johnson killed five cops in Dallas, Texas, not before. So, as you can see, I just wanted life for Blacks to improve somewhat, at least on the same scale as homosexuals. But it didn't happen. I know Obama was caught between a rock and a hard place, and it would not be *presidential* for him to show the entire country that he is putting the needs of one race before another. Still, he could have thrown in a couple of bills and regulations on the low-low before Whites found out. I'm just saying.

ANOTHER ONE
BITES THE DUST

Black men dying at the hands of white men is nothing new in this country; it has been happening for centuries. Nine times out of ten, the killings are racially motivated. What kind of motivation is it when black men kill other black men? Hmm. When slave owners killed male slaves, they were sending a message, mainly to the mothers. The only difference now is that the message is sent to the *entire* black community. Who cares if one of these cops is arrested for murder or for a lesser charge such as manslaughter? The initial indictment of these cops, as well as their trial, is usually a joke. A farce. A sham. A charade. A mockery of what our judicial system is supposed to be. Fair. Stop being delusional, black people. Their trial—-if the case goes to trial—- is nothing more than a pretense put on to temporarily appease the black community, because we all know 99.9% of them will never see the inside of a prison cell. Today, more white cops are arrested, including those cops who killed George Floyd. Some have even been convicted, and people around the world—-not just the country—-will be hanging on the edge of their seat to hear the outcome. Even though the majority of these cops deserve to be thrown under the jail, I still view their arrest as a means of temporarily calming the black community. How many more black men will white cops murder in the next 5 years? Ten years?

Centuries ago, the killing of our black men was murder and most of the killings today are murder, too; a badge and a uniform do not change a thing.

These killings have prompted city governments to defund police departments, but I do not think this is enough. As our president at the time and as a black man, Obama (who is still my guy) could have at least put a cap on the amount of black men white cops were allowed to kill in a single calendar year. And any department that went over its quota would be fined heavily, and the responsible cops would be terminated. Keep bringing money into the equation and I bet 95% of cops will use their tasers so much that taser-charging stations would pop up all across the country. How 'bout it?

IMMIGRANTS AND REFUGEES

Now, how many refugees did Obama allow into this country and how many more would Hillary have let in? I read that a refugee family moved into a 3-bedroom, 2-bath house in Pennsylvania in 2016. I don't know about you, but I know of several American families who could have benefitted from moving into that house. With the United States trillions of dollars in debt, can our government really afford to do this? Well, if it cannot afford to repair our schools, roads, and bridges, I think not. Because of Middle Eastern wars, these refugees are in dire need of housing, food, clothing, and healthcare, the same things our own poverty-stricken citizens need right now. Who is going to pay for all of these necessities? American taxpayers? Hmm. Immigrants who are here in the USA, legally or illegally, are eligible for free healthcare. Even if they are not eligible, they are still going to get it. There are some stipulations involved, but some immigrants can get health coverage easier than some American citizens can. Wow.

This just seems completely backwards; and it would be a downright shame to see refugees living better than thousands or millions of American-born citizens. And we cannot forget that for up to five years they are in the United States, *some* of them work tax free, while Americans have X amount of dollars taken out of every paycheck. The gross pay for many foreigners is actually their net pay. That's right folks; for about five years, they have zero taxes taken out of their pay! None! Now this only applies to certain *exempt individuals*, but millions of foreigners, including Latinos, have been capitalizing on this for decades. But don't blame them; blame our stupid government. Whether a U.S. citizen or not, foreigners—-any foreigners—-should be taxed exactly how Americans are taxed. Think about how this could help reduce the national debt instead of constantly raising taxes for us.

Have you ever worked somewhere for more than five years and noticed a particular Latino individual has come up missing? Six months goes by, maybe a year, and lo and behold, the guy is back...pumped and ready to work for another few years. Oh... what? You didn't know they could come back and do it again? Black people, stop being delusional. This is why so many Latinos and other foreigners flock to the United States. If this system is no longer in place, then our government had to have recently stopped it. I once saw a paycheck belonging to a man from the Philippines. He had been working in the US for about 18 months. Not one cent was taken out of his paycheck,- and he actually had the nerve to brag about it. Our government treats people from other countries better than its own citizens because it has to be receiving some very lucrative kickbacks. Again—-it's all about the money.

TAKING A PAGE
FROM HILLARY CLINTON

Many Americans believe Trump is a racist; true, but I believe Hillary is just as prejudice, if not more. She just does a better job at hiding it. But don't be fooled. In the 90's, Hillary had the nerve to call black youths (mainly gangbangers and drug dealers) "... super predators, without conscience or empathy." Is she kidding? White people are the super predators of this world, always have been, always will be.

Without conscience or empathy, our white government allowed white slumlords to get away with renting run-down, rat-infested apartments to black people; and turned a blind eye when rats maimed or killed a black infant.

Without conscience or empathy, our white government strategically planted one of the most addictive drugs in black neighborhoods to facilitate the termination of a race of people. They carried this out with the intent to create chaos. This is not any different from city officials allowing liquor stores to be built in black, low-income communities, as well as Latino communities. People, they purposely do this. Why? Because more drunk black people mean more black arrests, and more Blacks behind bars. Hell, they don't even have to be drunk. I know that anyone can easily drive to a store and buy a bottle, but the city makes it *more* convenient for us. Take the time to drive through a white, middle-class neighborhood and let me know how many liquor stores you see. (Drive quickly so the Caucasians don't have a chance to call the cops.) Whites do not want liquor stores in their neighborhood because these establishments bring down the property value. An older lady I am acquainted with owns a beautiful, well-maintained home. It could easily sell for over $100,000...if it was located in a well-maintained neighborhood. But it's not. Many of the homes next to her and across from her are nothing but big piles of trash, so she will be lucky if she gets $60,000 from the sale.

Without conscience or empathy, our white government conducted experiments on Blacks that left them blind, incapacitated, or dead.

Without conscience or empathy, our white government denied welfare benefits to many Blacks during the Great Depression.

Without conscience or empathy, white men hunt and kill Blacks for sport. Oh, what? You thought that movie with Ice-T (*Surviving the Game*) was made up? Please! This crap still occurs today! White people, *super predators*, love to kill. Plain and simple. Go ahead and keep believing this is just a conspiracy theory...if you want to. Think about it. With 1.5 million black men missing in America today, what do you think happened to them? There are several reasons why they are missing, including not wanting to be found; but the majority of us know that a large number of them are more than likely dead, or even victims of organ theft...mostly at the hands of Whites. The only other group that can close to comparison in terms of missing people is Native Americans; in fact, they just might surpass us.

Now let me give you one more.

Without conscience or empathy, Whites have systematically wiped out entire black towns; and I'm not even going to talk about what they did during slavery...well, not right now. And even though I shouldn't, I'm going to again mention white cops who are murdering black men by declaring they were in fear for their life, even if the assailant was unarmed, turned away from the cop, and at least 25 feet away. How does this not add up to murder? How is it that an unarmed black man can get shot seven times by one cop, but a white man who gunned down a dozen people makes it to jail without a single scratch? Unbelievable!

Some white cops are truly evil, and as Edmund Burke put it, "The only thing necessary for the triumph of evil is for good men to do nothing." I truly believe that Micah Johnson, ex-military gunman from Texas, was no longer willing to stand around and do nothing; but we can only speculate what was going on in his head before the shooting. PTSD or not, he probably viewed the injustice in this country as overtaking the good. And as one very famous man once said, "When injustice becomes law, resistance becomes duty." Perhaps Johnson felt it was his duty to resist what was happening to our young black men.

Cops kill black men not only because they have the authority to do so, but mainly because they want to. They know that they can easily shoot out a knee-cap, but they would rather shoot to kill. Many of them hide behind their badge and use it as a get-out-of-jail-free card because there are no real consequences for their actions. As my co-worker, Miss Rose, puts it: Law enforcement hasn't done nothing but substitute the noose for a 9mm. In my opinion, if some white cops had the opportunity to rewrite the law enforcement code on the side of their squad cars, instead of *To Protect and Serve*, the doors would read *To Kill and Eradicate*. Regrettably, the only time black men ever get a reprieve from white cops is after a *terrorist* situation (9/11 and the Boston Marathon). Am I right or wrong? But mark my words; the murder of unarmed black men by white cops may have slowed down somewhat, but it will never end...until we end it.

THE KKK

I would not be surprised at all if the KKK had orchestrated some of these killings from the very start. As I have been saying for years, the Klan may be silent, but it is not dormant. The Klan is also not stupid. It knows that it cannot operate as it once did decades ago: up close, in your face, and with no regard to the law. No. The Klan has a plan. There has been so little activity on the part of the Klan lately that it makes sense to believe they will eventually make a move. We don't know where and we don't know when; and this is very scary. But what's even scarier is the fact that Klansmen are everywhere. They are teachers, farmers, judges, preachers, doctors, janitors and mechanics, restaurant workers, police officers, and yes, White House officials. This is why I say they are not stupid. Many of them will not show their true colors in public; they will wait until they meet up at rallies with hoods to hide their identity. Make no mistake. They're out there, so watch your back.

MORE ON POLITICS

Bringing you back to the subject of politics, I also believe both Donald and Hillary are crooks, even if no one is willing to prove it. Trump has been accused of cheating hundreds of low-income people who worked for him; many of them minorities. He calls this "business." And I think he definitely has some shady dealings going on with Putin. Now, it sure was mighty convenient that before certain individuals were set to testify against the Clintons, these same individuals *came up dead*. Supporters of the Clintons, of course, rushed to say these were rumors made up by Russia to sabotage Hilary's campaign; but all the witnesses did die...*all* of them. If you do not know anything about this, look it up. Of course, it could be just a coincidence, witnesses dying around the same time *and before* they could testify in a court of law. Hmm. If you have ever watched the movie *Conspiracy Theory* with Mel Gibson and Julia Roberts, or the television series *Designated Survivor* with Keifer Sutherland, you will understand exactly what I'm talking about.

A conspiracy theory is "a belief that explains an event or set of circumstances as the result of a secret plot, usually by very powerful conspirators, and oftentimes in politics." Many of you will say, "Oh, it's just a movie." Where in the Hell do you think material for movies such as these comes from? It comes from real life. The British Intelligence Agency MI6 really does exist. Film companies use real ex-CIA agents and Navy Seals to consult on projects. The television series *Scandal* shows us how things work behind closed doors on

Capitol Hill. It is so true that some individuals who have a connection with the White House are shut down, bribed, blackmailed or murdered. This really does happen! It is the naïve people in this country who think such atrocities take place only in the mob or in gangs. This is exactly what occurred *before* and *during* Hillary's campaign for the presidency. But how would any of us know this?

Nearly every disgusting and corrupt move the Clintons made throughout the years, with the exception of Bill's tryst with Monica Lewinsky, was intentionally kept from the public by controlling the media, even her own "business" involvement with Russia's Vladimir Putin that had been going on for years. And who controls the media? Exactly! But not the internet! I'm sure many of you voted for Hillary; and although she did not become president, take the time to discover what kind of "super predator" you would have helped put in office. Let me tell you something. Stop believing everything you see and hear on the television, and stop being so delusional!

THE ERADICATION
OF BLACKS

Again, our young black men (and women) are still dying at the hands of police officers at a nearly unprecedented rate, especially from 2014 to 2016, and again from 2018 to 2020—-and the year is not even over yet. Never forget that white cops killed over 200 black men in 2016, and most of them were unarmed. Do you remember the shooting of Tamir Rice? Of course you do. Twelve years old and playing with a toy gun in the park—-by himself! Cops pulled up and shot him within a few seconds of exiting their vehicle.

Instead of a cop, a cop-wannabe killed Trayvon Martin. George Zimmerman was the one who stalked Martin; he shot him because he was also "in fear for his life." Oh, and we cannot forget about the 1991 tragic death of Latasha Harlins in Los Angeles, who was shot "execution style" in the head over a measly bottle of orange juice. The Korean store owner never did any prison time. Is this really the 21th century? Sometimes it's difficult to tell.

We can protest 'til the cows come home, but very little will ever get accomplished, particularly if we have a traitor in our midst. What I mean by this is that during peaceful protests organized by Blacks, chaos sometimes erupts because someone paid an individual to intentionally disrupt the demonstration. It could be the government, racist Whites, or the media. This action makes black people look violent and provides the media with "breaking news" footage. White people are helping the cause but some of them are hindering it. Oftentimes this "traitor" is a black person who is willing to betray his own race for a lousy few hundred dollars. Sad.

Think about 1916 Waco, Texas, where Jesse Washington was castrated and burned alive in front of a crowd of 15,000 Whites. That was 15,000 bloodthirsty, *super predators* eagerly waiting to watch a black man get his nut-sack cut off! The townsfolk found Washington guilty of murdering the wife of his boss. There is no doubt in my mind that Jesse's boss killed his own wife and framed Jesse, who was slightly mentally challenged and only 17 years old. Wow. It's so very sad, but I often feel that the only safe place for our black men is behind bars. This is a horrible thing to say, I know, but at least more of them would be alive. But take note, people; black-on-black crime is just as senseless as Blacks being murdered by white cops! Either way, we are still losing our black brothers.

A DIFFERENT TYPE
OF ERADICATION?

A few black activists believe the eradication of blacks also stems from the founder of Planned Parenthood. Margaret Sanger started Planned Parenthood around 1939, although the establishment was originally called the Birth Control Federation of America (BCFA) for the first three years. I have mixed feelings about Sanger's efforts when it comes to her trying to help Blacks; but after some extensive reading in academic journals, I actually believe others were involved in the intent to diminish the black race. Sanger said that birth control was created to accomplish this:

> "...to help a group notoriously underprivileged and handicapped to a large measure by a 'caste' system that operates as an added weight upon their efforts to get a fair share of the better things in life."

This was especially true in the South because many poor Blacks had soaring birth rates, but their quality of life was far below substandard.

After Sanger teamed up with Mary Reinhardt from the BCFA, the two wrote a statement saying, "Negroes present the great problem of the South, as they are the group with the greatest economic, health, and social problems."

The two of them outlined a practical birth control program geared toward a population characterized as largely illiterate and that "still breeds carelessly and disastrously." Now, before you get your panties in a bunch, you need to know that W.E.B. Dubois, a black man, made these comments, not Sanger. Dubois's entire comment went something like this:

The mass of ignorant Negroes still breed carelessly and disastrously, so that the increase among Negroes, even more than the increase among Whites, is from that part of the population *least* intelligent and fit, and *least* able to rear their children properly.

I hate to say it, but we still have Blacks who fall into this category today; and it still doesn't make any sense.

It seems as if Reinhardt got ahead of herself, and Sanger quickly lost control of her own project. From the start, Sanger wanted black ministers and doctors to lead this project, so black communities would be more trusting and become more involved. She was totally against white doctors supplying contraceptives to black women, but this is exactly what happened. Sanger wanted to educate black females on contraceptives, but the whites in charge felt that this was a waste of time. For the most part, the project ended up resembling a vaccination camp.

Even today, Sanger comes across as a racist, as a Hitler wannabe. I believe this is because of the horrendous actions Planned Parenthood has been known to do. Planned Parenthood harvests fetuses on a daily basis and sells them to the highest bidders known as Tissue Procurers. Research facilities use baby tissue, liver, and other parts to create vaccines for rubella and chickenpox, to treat Parkinson's disease, and a host of other illnesses. An undercover video (plam.org/planned-parenthood-harvests-baby-parts/) aired on the news not too long ago and showed the unethical practices of Planned Parenthood doctors. My point for bringing this to your attention is the fact that black females have three times as many abortions as white females and about twice as many as Latinas. These rates were the other way around from the 70's to the 90's. Then I guess some black females just lost their ever-loving mind.

Ladies, how difficult is it to get on birth control? Abortion is yet another way for Whites to profit off Blacks, and we keep allowing them to do it. This tissue procuring is inhumane and is supposed to be illegal; and doctors are required to get the mother's consent for this procedure. Do you think they have stopped since reporters exposed them? I seriously doubt it. In fact, I bet they haven't skipped a beat. I found out that a black female in California had approximately seven abortions in less than three years. Wow. That's a lot. I wonder if she is getting a share of the corporation's profits.

Now, this practice of using fetuses has been going on since the 1930's. Doesn't it make you wonder why other Whites were so eager to take over Sanger's project around this same time? It's all about what?...the money. With Hillary Clinton firmly backing Planned Parenthood, despite the damning videos, she was able to obtain its endorsement for her campaign. I wonder if Hillary has shares in Planned Parenthood. Hmm.

THE SEPARATION OF BLACKS

I have heard some black activists allege that Blacks are the most lost race of people on earth. I can believe this to some extent; but only because a large number of us do not value family the way we should, and the way we used to. When it comes to family members working as a single entity, we need to take a page from the Asians and Latinos. We all laugh when we hear a comedian joke about a Mexican or Latino family of twelve living in a 2-bedroom, 1-bath house; but with nearly all the adults bringing home a paycheck, they're handling their business, oftentimes without receiving a single penny in government assistance! Many of them use their hard-earned money to buy new vehicles in cash, instead of making monthly payments. They sometimes do the same when buying a house or at least have a large down payment, so their monthly mortgage is as low as possible.

I know a guy who does nothing but boast about the cost of his house and the fact that his mortgage is $2,000 a month. Can you say house poor?... because that's exactly what he is. His new house is nothing but a financial drain and he is struggling. What Latinos and Asians do is exactly what we need to do; we need to work with one another instead of against one another! How 'bout it?

Better yet, take a page from the Nigerians, especially those living in the city of Lagos. My husband and I watched Anthony Bourdain's *Parts Unknown: Lagos* one Sunday night, and were amazed at the resiliency and optimism of these people. An entire city of around 14 million and none of them pity their situation or complain about not being able to find a job. Instead, they have the mindset of "What can I *learn* to do that will support my family?" They make jewelry by hand, shoes by hand, cook all types of delicacies and sell them, and teach themselves how to repair computers, laptops, and cell phones. In fact, they can take a cell phone apart and put it back together in a matter of minutes. They do all this without a college education and are totally self-sufficient. Education is a top priority to them and all the children go to school. What's really amazing is that *no one* receives government assistance and no one pays taxes. Wow. The people of Nigeria work together and not against one another; and they have absolutely no concept of what it is to be lazy.

OUR GOVERNMENT KNOWS
HOW TO CREATE CHAOS
AMONG BLACKS

One thing our government has always been successful in doing is creating chaos among black people. How does it accomplish this? One way is through skin tone. We see it every day on the television in commercials, TV series, and even on billboards. This is one of the best ways to keep us separate from one another. Too many of us are petty and waste time knocking children of interracial couples. Do not knock them for following their Caucasian side; they have every right to choose their own path. No one can expect individuals who are the product of two races, one of them black, to automatically embrace the black side. Influence is what counts in situations such as these. So please, give these children and adults a break, and stop belittling them for not embracing the roots of their black parent.

Now, this separation actually began during slavery, by allowing most of the light-skinned Blacks to work in the house, while the majority of *darkies* kept to the fields. C'mon, people! If we do not get ourselves on the same page, then we will never come together as a defining force. The government is afraid of this happening because it does not want all Blacks to become self-sufficient, similar to most Asians and Latinos. Now, most states generate a lot of federal funding because of low-income individuals. The Nigerian government once attempted to take over Lagos, but the people were not having it. Never forget how afraid our government was of the Black Panthers, who also created a self-sufficient community; and how low our government stooped to rid the country of them. Our government would rather have us remain docile and dependent, just like our slave ancestors. If it weren't for the heat and the bugs, I'd probably move to Nigeria.

GOVERNMENT CONTROL

Too many people believe that anything they can get for free is better. This is not always the case, especially when *free* does not constitute *freedom*. There was a guy named Saul Alinsky who died in the 70's. He had some pretty radical ideas, but I liked them. He talked about the eight methods of government control, the kind of control our government has over us...some more than others.

Number One: Control healthcare and you control the people. Wow. Sound familiar? Medicaid. Obamacare: Government healthcare with a penalty.

Number Two: Increase the poverty level as high as possible; poor people are easier to control and will not fight back if *you* (slave owner or the government, take your pick) are providing *everything* for them (medical, food (Link), and subsidized housing). Hmm.

Did you know there were more black, middle-class families during the 80's than there are today? This changed drastically after the NAFTA deal. Our government intentionally *helped* black people into poverty. Notice that I said *helped* because the government did not do it alone. Many of us had a hand in our own downfall. We just refuse to see it.

Number Three: Increase the debt to an *unsustainable* level. That way, *you* (the government) are able to increase taxes, and this will produce more poverty. This is what our politicians do nearly every year. They keep chipping away at our paycheck, making it smaller and smaller every time we turn around. In July of 2017, my husband noticed that his paycheck was short by 7 dollars. It seems that hard working Americans always have to pay for our government's stupidity.

Number Four: Make gun control a priority and *remove* the ability to defend themselves from the government. When individuals acquire a felony in many states, they automatically lose their ability to own a firearm. That way *you* are able to create a police state. Now hold on, people! I gotta break this one down for those of you who do not realize the severity of this action.

This is exactly what was happening during slavery. The ability for slaves to defend themselves was *removed*. People, get a gun license and start stockpiling weapons. White folks do it all the time. Now, a *police state* is a totalitarian state controlled by a political police force (the government) that secretly *supervises* the activities of citizens. A *totalitarian* system of government is centralized and dictatorial (as in having absolute control and authority over a country), and requires complete subservience by the people (the same as total obedience from a slave). Most of us, regardless of color, will be at the mercy of the government if we are without firepower.

Now, a lot of you may think that a government like this could never develop in the United States, but guess what? You're wrong. The reason I say this is because of a little old article called 13603. It is actually referred to as Executive Order 13603, and guess who signed off on it in 2012? Obama. Article 13603 was put in place for National Defense Resources Preparedness. Of course, every country wants to be prepared for any type of threat or disaster, and Sec. 102 of the article shows this concern:

The United States must have an industrial and technological base capable of meeting national defense requirements and capable of contributing to the technological superiority of its national defense equipment in peacetime and in times of national emergency. The authorities provided in the Act shall be used to strengthen this base and to ensure it is capable of responding to the national defense needs of the United States.

Sec. 103 E states that "Executive departments and agencies {will} foster cooperation between the defense and commercial sectors for research and development and for *acquisition* of materials, services, components, and equipment to enhance industrial base efficiency and responsiveness."

In case you do not know, *acquisition* means the act of acquiring something, such as property or skilled laborers. Stay with me now. Sec. 201 gets me a little closer to my point: "...to allocate materials, services, and facilities as deemed necessary or appropriate to promote the national defense." It doesn't sound too bad, right? But let me tell you *how* our government plans on implementing this strategy.

Sec. 502 states that "The head of each agency otherwise delegated functions under this order is delegated the authority of the President [...], to employ persons of outstanding experience and ability *without compensation...*"

Let me say that one more time. "...without compensation." Executive Order 13603 gives heads of government agencies the authority to confiscate our property, our home, our food, and even make us work without compensation, all for the *good* of national defense. Who in the world is going to work without pay? Oh, yeah...slaves. Although Obama is gone, this Executive order is still in place. Wow. So, imagine a nationwide disaster or foreign threat to this country. All that food you took the time to grow, and the days and weeks you spent canning can be confiscated by our government. The guns and rifles you paid thousands of dollars for will be taken away in the blink of an eye. Will you get your guns back? Probably not, and if you are not Luke Cage or Black Panther, then you're going to need some guns.

Number Five: Promote welfare. Take control of every aspect of their lives (food, housing, and income). C'mon, people! You know this is just another form of slavery! Slave owners controlled every aspect of the lives of our ancestors, and the government has found it *so* easy to continue with this tradition. The government gives you a certain amount on your Link card, free medical care (with stipulations), and a place to live for next to nothing. But for the most part, these benefits can only be had if you *EARN* next to nothing! Go above the standard, poverty income level and these benefits will disappear like they were never there. My black people! Stop being so delusional! This is how the government controls your income. If your income is controlled, it makes it extremely difficult to ever get out of poverty! If you never leave poverty, then you will never come close to being a part of the middle class—-exactly where the government *doesn't* want us to be!

Number Six: Education. Take control of what people read and listen to, and take control of what children learn in school. Now, this might not apply very much to today's modern world because no matter what is taught in the classroom, kids can discover just about anything they want by going online.

Not so when I was growing up in the 70's and early 80's. Education for Blacks was so limited in the classroom, and it was an education more advantageous to Whites than any other color. It was even worse for Blacks in the 50's, when more public schools for us started springing up across the nation. Our wonderful president at the time, Eisenhauer, intentionally made sure the curriculum for black kids was second-rate to Whites. I will talk more on this subject later.

Number Seven: Remove the belief in God from the government and schools. Been there. Done that.

Number Eight: Class Warfare. Divide the people into the wealthy and the poor. This will cause more discontent, and it will be easier to *take* the wealthy (tax them) with the support of the poor. The part about discontentment I can believe, especially in this country; but to actually think that taxing the wealthy is an easy thing to do is absolutely ridiculous. Ask Trump how much he paid in taxes last year. Exactly!

RELIGION

Let me get back to Number Seven. I have spoken to many people throughout my life and asked them why they do not attend church. Some said they could not find a church that was a good fit for them; but the majority of them believe that pastors, preachers, and church deacons are corrupt and greedy. They also say that people of different denominations spend too much time criticizing other religions, constantly claiming that biblical events happened according to *their* version, not another's. The fact is *no one* living today has an inkling of exactly how these events took place, because anyone alive right now was not alive 2,000 years ago! How 'bout it?

Black evangelists are in the perfect position to organize and lead their congregation against the tyranny of the government and white cops, as well as motivate people to lead a better life. Instead, some *men of God* are too worried about whether or not their ATM in the lobby is working properly. An ATM in a church lobby? Wow! Now, I am not a religious person, but I do know that the Bible says that the clergy are supposed to be of humble means. Yet Creflo Dollar is worth around 30 million dollars, owns more than one home, a couple of Rolls Royces, and a jet. If that's not enough, he had the nerve to ask his congregation (many of them in the low-income bracket) to donate their hard-earned money just so he can upgrade to a bigger and better jet. He said a new jet would allow him to better spread the word of God. Really? Last time I checked the Bible, in order for Jesus to spread the Word of God, he *walked* the earth. Creflo had better download the app for MarcoPolo or Skype. How 'bout it?

Get this. A childhood friend of mine started attending the church I went to when I was growing up. One day, the elders informed her that her membership had been revoked because she was not "contributing" to the church to their satisfaction. I guess her measly two or three dollars a week was an insult to them. Wow. Do any of you believe that Jesus would have turned away any individual who could not pay? I think not. Black people are so delusional. Don't think I'm knocking your religion because I'm not. But I am knocking those who are *capitalizing* from your religion, and I just want you to see it. Go eight Sundays in a row without putting money in the collection plate and see what happens. Hmm.

PLAIN IGNORANCE

Now, part of this discontentment stems from a large portion of black society not encouraging its own to get off welfare. Tell me this. Why is it that Tyrone, down the street, can tell me how to swindle the Social Security Administration into giving me a disability check (when I'm perfectly capable of performing physical labor), yet he has no idea how to fill out a personal check? Why is it that Shanika, around the corner, encourages her younger sister to keep having children just so her Link will increase; yet she had her own children taken away by DCFS? Why is it that when Shanika's 6-year-old daughter plays house with the neighborhood kids, she does not portray a kind and loving mother? Instead, she sounds something like this: Get your m***** f*****' a** in da house! And stop cryin' like a little b****! If you don't shut the f*** up, I'm gonna beat da s*** outta you! These are the actual words of a 6-year-old girl that came floating through my window more than twenty-five years ago. Make no mistake; I have heard white parents speak to their children in the same way; but this book is not about them; it's about us. What's even sadder about Shanika's *style* of play is that all the other kids went right along with her like nothing was wrong, like nothing was out of the ordinary with the little girl's version of *house*. I stood by the window waiting for just one of the children to speak up, to declare they were playing house incorrectly; but not one of them said a word. Wow! I used to play house with the neighborhood kids when I was growing up, but our make-believe never sounded so harsh or so sad. Not one kind word came out of this girl's mouth during make-believe. I have always wondered if she grew up to have children of her own, and if she talks to them in the same way. But who do you suppose this little girl was imitating when she was playing house? Her mother. This was all the girl knew because her "loving" mother spoke to her in the same tone of voice, and used the same foul words. At six years of age, most children respond to the tone of a parent's voice, not the words. It will be a totally different ball game when Shanika's daughter discovers the true meaning of these words as she gets older. Why do situations such as these continue to occur in the black community? Well, as my son says, "It's all about common sense, but common sense ain't common." I have to agree because if it were, everyone would have it. How 'bout it?

CYCLES IN THE BLACK FAMILY

Irst and foremost, certain family lifestyles are nothing but cycles. Children usually emulate whatever their parents do and this is often repeated throughout each generation. Boys who grow up without a dad often find it easy to distance themselves from any children they happen to father. At the same time, there are some boys in the same situation who grow up vowing to always be in their children's life; they do not want their kids to experience the same fate. More power to them.

It's because we create these cycles; we find complacency in them; and some of us allow them to continue because we *choose* not to follow a different path. It's also because too many of us would rather stay drunk and high, instead of helping our children with their homework, or showing them what hard work really is. It's because some of us would rather let our children flunk kindergarten or the first grade, instead of taking the time to enroll them in summer school. It's because we choose to remain ignorant instead of getting an education, whether self-taught or in a school, thereby preventing ourselves from excelling in life. This falls in line with *dumbing down*, and many of you know what I'm talking about. Quite of few of us pretend to be dumb and put on a façade of ignorance, just to fit in with certain black people. Let me tell you what I'm talking about.

By the time my daughter got to the 5ᵗʰ grade, she was on the honor roll and played the clarinet in band; she also got A's in science and math. I made sure she knew how proud of her I was. The teachers used to call home just to sing her praises. All that changed in one week. Literally. She purposely began to fail her classes, and started yelling and cursing at her teachers. She even started speaking as if she had been born and bred on a plantation, *intentionally* misusing words and giving them two syllables when they have only one. When I asked her what was going on, she replied, "I'm tired of being called a nerd." Wow. Peer pressure from other black children got to her and she caved in. My daughter did a complete one-eighty, simply so kids of her own race would stop thinking of her as a nerd and be her friend. Stop being so delusional, black people. Where is this dumbing down going to get you? If you are an exceptionally smart individual, then use your intelligence to secure your future and the future of your children. Remember, a mind is a terrible thing to waste.

LANGUAGE

If I talk about education, then I have to talk about language. If I talk about language, then I have to talk about the misuse of particular words. People, listen up. Never start a sentence with *Is you* or *Was you*. It's *Are you* or *Were you*. The words *looked* and *liked* are one syllable, not two. They should not be pronounced *like-tid* or *look-tid*. And we do not say, "That's mines." Instead, say, "That's mine." And there is no such word as *worser*. It's *bad, worse,* and *worst* (Last night was the *worst* date I ever had). That's it. Many of you might not realize that this is how our ancestors spoke when they were on the plantation. "Is ya goin' ta town taday, Massuh?" I hear parents and grandparents speaking like this, young adults, teens, and children as young as three. This dialect should be dead and buried, and there is absolutely no reason for any of us to speak this way 150 years after slavery ended. Yet we still do. Sad.

Look. I'm not naïve. I know there are a lot of black people in this country who do not care about their speech (and they are probably cussing me out big time right about now). They don't want to appear bougie in any way. But I have to let you know that the way we speak can sometimes hinder us in our place of employment, even keep us from landing a particular job. Let me tell you what I mean by this. When I was a teenager, I got a job at a fast-food restaurant. Two employees were up for the supervisor position. Both were black females who were very nice; they had a good attendance record, and got along great with everyone. They also had been working at the restaurant for approximately the same length of time. The only difference between the two was the way they spoke. One spoke correct English; while the other, let's call her Karen, sounded like she was a cousin of Kizzy's, (*Roots)* twice removed. She practically butchered the English language every time she opened her mouth, as well as spat out big words she had no idea how to use correctly. Of course, the other female got the position, and the manager never told Karen why she had been passed over. The rest of us knew why. It's simple. Most owners and managers do not want employees representing their business if they do not act right, look right, or speak right. It's the same with people who are covered in tattoos. They would blend in just fine at a car repair shop; but at the front end of certain restaurants, they would have to wear long sleeves.

Our names can sometimes have the same negative effect on future employment. I eventually went from working in fast-food restaurants to sit-down restaurants. One day after a lunch rush, the managers sat down at one of the tables to sort through a pile of applications. As I walked past them, I noticed that they had made two piles. I could hear one of them say the names on each application out loud, and then put them in one of the two piles. This is what I heard:

> "Shaquwonda...nope. Quantierra...nope.
> Amberdette...nope. Taquassha...nope."

Of course, all of these applicants went into a pile by themselves. I worked at this restaurant for 5 years and never came across employees with these names. Hmm.

MORE ON CYCLES

These recurring cycles are also because we choose to have more children than we are capable of taking care of financially. These cycles exist when black parents allow their children to watch television shows that are way too mature for them, the type of shows that are derogatory and only present the ignorant and uneducated side of Blacks. I will use the TV series *Bad Girls Club* to make my case in point. This show is about sex and fighting, nothing else! I was in someone's home where I actually saw a 4-year-old girl watching this show. Are you kidding me? Not all Blacks want their race portrayed in this light. Sidney Poitier, 90 years old and an exceptional actor, refused to take on acting roles that diminished his character and made his race look stupid, even though he was poor and struggling to put food on the table for his family. Check out his portrayal of a strong black man in the movies *Buck and the Preacher* and *In The Heat of the Night*.

These cycles also persist because we choose not to educate our impressionable young children on their black heritage, or show them how proud we are to be Black. It's because some of us cuss our children out as if they were some mangy dog on the street, instead of providing them with positive guidance. And it's because some of us choose to depend more on a corrupt government than our own capabilities. It's never-ending until one family member decides to stop the cycle and try something new.

THE HEALTHCARE ISSUE

We all know that it does not matter that more Whites receive government assistance than any other race in this country. *Mainstream society* still views Blacks and Latinos as a strain on the country's budget; and feels as if many of us do not pay our fair share of taxes, or sees us as a bunch of lazy human beings. I have actually come across a few white people who refuse to believe that their race receives more state benefits than Blacks do. I just told them to look it up.

Most white taxpayers in this country do not care if we cannot pay our rent or do not have enough money to buy some much needed medicine for our sick child. When I think of individuals who do not have the money to pay for certain prescription drugs, I cannot help but think about how the rich outlive the poor, especially poor minorities. Then this makes me think about the EpiPen, which cost roughly around $600 when it first hit the market. Families with upper-middle class incomes and, of course, the wealthy, could easily afford to pay this price. But what about low-income families without healthcare, the ones who cannot really afford health insurance but do not qualify for state assistance? How could they possibly pay such a high price? Do you think pharmaceutical companies care? Not one bit. Whether low-income people can afford to pay for the pen or not, CEOs and presidents of these companies still get paid. It was a miracle that the government, or whoever, stepped in on this issue.

In all likelihood, the price of healthcare in the United States is going to skyrocket in the following years, making it even more difficult for hard working Americans to afford it. One good thing Trump is attempting to do is get rid of the penalty for not having health insurance. Let's see if he sticks to his word. Penalizing the American people was one of the dumbest moves Obama ever made. Where was the fairness in this? The government has been penalizing us for decades, as if it's our fault this country is in debt. If people could so easily afford health insurance, they would probably have it. It's pretty difficult for some of us to dish out $200 a month for decent health insurance and still make ends meet when they are earning only $8.50 an hour. Oh, there is health insurance available for just $65 a month, but it comes with a $5,000 deductible.

On the other hand, Trump thinks he is slick by increasing our paychecks. For just a little while, things are going to seem great. More money in our pockets means more buying and spending. Yeah! Then, out of nowhere—-BOOM! Inflation, rising gas prices, and mortgage rates. And we find ourselves right back where we started. What Trump is doing is *the underlay for the overplay*. How 'bout it? Our wonderful government never gives taxpayers something for nothing. Do you still think the government cares about you? Let me tell you how much.

GOVERNMENT MANEUVERS

This goes far beyond what the real "super predators" in this country did to slaves. This goes beyond the lynching of our parents and grandparents in the early 20th century; and this goes beyond the tragedies that occurred in the 1960's. Let's first talk about farming. Have any of you ever wondered what happened to the black farmers of America? Yeah, believe it or not, there are black farmers in this country; but there are not enough. Why is that? Because their land was stolen from them by incensed Whites and the racist USDA. A government agriculture website says that around 1920, there were almost a million farms owned and operated by Blacks. This was millions of farmland that, when combined, equaled the size of New Hampshire, New Jersey, and Massachusetts. Out of all American farmers, Blacks amounted to 14%. Today, the total number of black farmers is less than 2%. Wow. Once you learn what happened, it won't be difficult to understand why the numbers have dwindled so much.

In the early part of the 20th century, black farmers had to deal with economic hardship, more so than Whites. The racist USDA constantly denied black farmers loans; but when they were able to get one, it was often much less than what white farmers received and repeatedly came too late in the season to do any planting. Because there was nothing even close to equal opportunity in those days, banks were able to swoop down on black farmers in the guise of a foreclosure. Even worse, many black families were run off their land by Whites. The Ku Klux Klan, *Super Predator* 5.0, definitely had a hand in this. They burned down homes, and the blood of Blacks spilt as murderous Whites drove them off. These same people rebuilt the houses and took over the land, sometimes in a matter of days because of those good, old-fashioned, barn-raisings. Many black families did not bother to seek help from local authorities because they, too, were often involved in the conspiracy. Not only did black families lose their land, but they often walked away with just the clothes on their back. Wow.

What about Bombingham? Oops, I mean Birmingham. What about Anna, Illinois, whose name (A.N.N.A.) is an acronym for "Ain't No Niggers Allowed." What about the events that took place in Tulsa, Oklahoma, in 1921, that has become a major topic of interest among the Black Lives Matter movement? This may remind some of you of the movie *Rosewood*. A section called Greenwood, aka Black Wall Street, was the home of thousands of flourishing, middle-class, black families. They had just about everything they needed: churches, theaters, stores, two newspapers, homes with running water, and better schools than most of the Whites, who lived across the tracks. Do you think these *super predators* liked this? Of course not. Whites were envious and resented seeing Blacks better off than they were, especially when many white men were having a difficult time finding work. Eventually, this resentment turned to hatred; and before these folks knew what was happening, Whites began murdering black men left and right, mostly by lynch mobs. The KKK led some of these mobs, which at the time was about 2,000 strong in the Tulsa area.

Many historians discovered that white men from Tulsa murdered black men because they had *attacked* a white woman (the same scenario in the movie *Rosewood*), and it was in the headlines the next morning. Please. We all know these *super predators* used this as an excuse to kill black people ("It was a nigger!"), very much in the same way white cops today use "I was in fear for my life." Well let me tell you; *all* the black citizens of Greenwood were in fear for their life on that fateful day. In less than 24 hours, nearly every home and business owned by Blacks was set on fire at the hands of angry white men; and thousands of Blacks were arrested, and hundreds were killed. A pregnant woman was unable to escape the chaos, and an angry white mob captured her. These *super predators* tied her to a stake and lit her on fire like the Salem Puritans did during the witch trials. If this is not horrific enough, they sliced open her stomach and stomped on her unborn baby as soon as it hit the ground. I don't know about you; but *whatever* young gangbangers and drug dealers do, or have done, cannot come close in comparison to what Whites have done to Blacks. How 'bout it?

Although some Blacks stood up to the white mobs, desperately trying to defend themselves and their homes, they were hopelessly outnumbered and outgunned; and had no other choice but to flee Tulsa. Their homes and businesses were bombed from the air by *flying super predators*, using dynamite and nitroglycerin! When the National Guard showed up the next morning, things did not get any better. Hundreds of more Blacks were arrested while Whites were left untouched. The white citizens of Tulsa blamed the devastation on the Greenwood Blacks, and that was all it took, the word of a white man over the word of a black one. End of story. That's not quite true. I forgot to explain why Blacks had trouble rebuilding Greenwood. Get this. These jealous *super predators* fabricated bogus ordinances to keep Blacks from rebuilding in their own district. Some of the Greenwood citizens were able to flourish for another 30 years, until the construction of the interstate pushed them out. Oh, I'm still not finished.

In 1906, in Atlanta, reports about black men assaulting and raping white women began appearing in two local newspapers. Again, this was more than likely another invented accusation by Whites to *justifiably* murder Blacks. Look what happened to Emmett Till. Supposedly, all he did was whistle at a white woman. Also in this area, many black citizens were thriving in farming and in business. Friction between Blacks and Whites really began to boil over, once black men gained the privilege to vote. Of course, Whites did not like this, especially the candidates, because black votes could possibly determine the outcome of an election. Candidates put fear into white voters by making them believe that Blacks could somehow undermine the status quo in society. *Undermine the status quo in society??* Yeah, right. Like that could ever happen. It is 2020 and our ability to disrupt the status quo in this country still hasn't happened.

So, what do you think transpired next? The same thing that always happens. Local newspapers printed stories about white women getting raped by black men. Once again, chaos broke out; Whites attacked Blacks, and about 40 of our people were murdered.

I have two questions for tragic events such as these: First, why call these events *race riots*, instead of what they really were? Massacres. My definition of a riot is two sides coming together *willingly* to duke it out. This is simply our government's attempt at trying to downplay the *super predatorness* of their parents and grandparents. Second, why couldn't Whites come up with an original excuse to justify attacking Blacks? There are so many incidents in history just like these that I could go on for another hundred pages; but I won't. How 'bout just one more.

For those of you who do not know, Rosewood is an actual town in the state of Florida; and the movie *Rosewood*, though very good, omitted so much of the senseless violence because it probably would have started a *real* race riot. I bet you can't guess how this one started. You probably think it was a white woman accusing a black man of rape? You got it. It really was the *same* lame excuse. The accusations came from a desperate white woman who had to explain to her husband where she had gotten the bruises on her face. What's an easy way to get yourself out of trouble? Blame it on a black man. Susan Smith did. It was the first thing that came out of her mouth. I do not have to go into much detail about what occurred in 1923, but black people lost everything, including their lives. One of my relatives was a victim of this type of conspiracy. Way back in the day, he was involved with a white woman. When their relationship was discovered, the woman cried rape. The law threw him in prison where he suffered needlessly for many long years. When he got out, he was a completely different man.

Now, this wonderful country of ours took 70 long years to give reparations to the survivors of the *Rosewood Massacre*, not the Race Riots of Rosewood, as it is referred to in the history books. Of course, there were not many of them left alive after seven decades, which I'm sure was fine with our government, seeing as how they did not have to dish out very much money. Those few who were still alive received about $150,000 each. Wow. And of course, not one single White was ever charged with murder.

CONFEDERATE FLAG REMOVAL

When most black people hear of tragedies such as these, they sometimes get themselves worked up over Confederate flags and statues, as many individuals have been doing of late. This controversy has been an issue in the South for many years; but no matter how we look at it, these things are still a part of Southern history. Don't let it get to you, people. Whether or not state governments remove the statues (and some have) or put them in museums, they are still going to be around. Sometimes it is beneficial for us to see Confederate flags in front of homes or on car windshields. This way, we can tell the friendlies from the enemies, and stay away from them. Do not stress over this too much because in about 75 to 100 years from now, Whites in this country will become the new minority. Many of us will not be around a century later, but our great-grandchildren will be able to take advantage of this. Hopefully.

FBI AND CIA ERADICATION PLANS
OF BLACK NEIGHBORHOODS AND
THE BLACK PANTHERS

Fast forward a few decades past 1920 and we have the illustrious FBI, the CIA, and their wonderful treatment of Blacks. Our country, our caring government, allowed J. Edgar Hoover—-no—-gave him its blessing to systematically destroy black leaders and black communities. The CIA went about this by flooding poor black communities with heroin. Bags filled with heroin were literally *dropped* on the sidewalk in black neighborhoods. What was the plan? Only to get Blacks addicted to heroin, to make them crave and care only about heroin, and to make them steal and murder for heroin. Guess what? Their plan backfired...big time. Yes, Blacks who became addicted to heroin did all the things that the CIA expected them to; but when Whites got a taste of heroin... that was all she wrote. Several years later, our government came up with the War on Drugs, not because *we* were strung out, but because white people were.

For the last several years, we have heard about the opioid epidemic that's wrecking this country; but what do you expect when pharmaceutical companies send 9 million hardcore, prescription drugs to a small town with a population of less than 400? The town is in West Virginia and the state has the highest death rate for overdoses in the entire nation. Why do 400 residents need 9 million OxyContin and Vicodin pills over the course of two years? If you do the math, this means that each person in this town gets more than 22,000 pills. There is only one pharmacy in town, yet thousands of people from surrounding counties flocked to it each week and often received more than one bottle of pills at a time. What's really going on?

Trump had the nerve to blame Mexico for bringing these pills into the United States when he knew damn well Americans were behind this—-American doctors and American wholesalers. Again, Trump was trying to divert the American people's attention away from the real culprits. Many pharmaceutical companies manufacture opioids right here in the United States and they, with the help of unethical doctors, led the public to believe that as long as opioids were used to treat pain, patients would not become addicted to them. Yeah, right. They knew these drugs were additive from the get go. This is no different from tobacco companies in the 1950's telling the public that cigarettes did not cause cancer. Everyone knows this was a lie. Again, it's always about what? The money.

Now some of you have to question why doctors and pharmaceutical companies would do something like this. I had to question it, too; I wanted to know who benefits from all these deaths. Well, the pharmaceutical companies and doctors are in it for the money, and so are politicians. Rep. Tom Marino, who, for a hot second, was endorsed by Trump for the position of drug czar, helped pass a law that *enabled* pharmaceutical companies and doctors to distribute millions of opioids, with a lot less interference from the DEA. If our government is so dedicated to the War on Drugs, why hinder the efforts of the DEA? Coincidentally, Marino and other politicians received thousands of dollars in campaign contributions from the same pharmaceutical companies; some received six-figure "gifts." Hmm. I would love to call them payoffs but that would be slander.

Just when the opioid epidemic was about at its highest, these politicians found a way to block the DEA's attempts to stop, or at least slow down illegal distribution. Marino had the nerve to say that the DEA was making it difficult for patients to obtain their much needed medicine. I'd like to say a few cuss words right about now, but I won't; but I will tell you why. Our wonderful government sends black men to prison, some for 25 to life, for selling drugs, even marijuana. When is the last time, *if ever*, you heard of someone overdosing on marijuana? Exactly! And we cannot forget about the states who have legalized marijuana. Luckily, Marino bowed out of the running for drug czar. It amazes me how some politicians are so corrupt, yet they don't get into a lick of trouble.

Who else benefits from all these people overdosing on opioids? Employers. For those of you who are skeptical about this, let me ask you one thing. Have you ever heard of Dead Peasant Insurance? Well, this is an insurance policy nearly 30% of all big companies have on their employees. Life insurance policies can range from $30,000 to the six-figure range, maybe higher. Some employers will increase the policy amount if their employees are prone to sickness or have opioid prescriptions. They're not stupid. They know that some people who take opioid medication will eventually become addicted and possibly OD. Once the employee dies, the payout is given to top executives in the form of bonuses. And guess what? Many employers keep the policy active, years after the employee leaves the company. So, there are quite a few employers in this country who would like nothing more than for this opioid epidemic to continue.

BACK TO THE CIA

The CIA has always been one of the biggest drug cartels in the country—-Hell, we might as well say the world. There was already a heroin epidemic in Vietnam during the war; even some American soldiers became heroin addicts. After witnessing the devastation heroin had caused among the Vietnamese people, our government confiscated large quantities and transported them to the United States. Next thing you know, heroin made landfall in poor, black neighborhoods. I would have loved to learn more about this in school when I was growing up. Labeling the CIA as a drug cartel is not slander because the agency's drug-dealing activities are actually public knowledge. You can find the information on the internet or at a library. Of course, our government intentionally kept these activities out of the history books, just like all the great accomplishments of Blacks, as well as the countless massacres of Blacks. But why? Well, for several reasons. The first one was to make sure that the actions of certain Whites never became public knowledge to the rest of white America. Another reason (for me) was to block the efforts of the black race from advancing. We had our *place* and we needed to stay in it. Cross-dressing Hoover and his cronies came up with various means in which to do this. They put lies in the newspapers about our positive black leaders to discredit them and put their integrity into question. These leaders were set up and framed for various crimes, so they would not be able to lead black communities.

Regardless of color, the American people would have to be downright stupid to think the FBI and other agencies in our government were innocent in the murder of some of our black leaders. When it came to the Black Panthers, Hoover's main objective was to insure "no messiah" could ever rise from the Panther Party; and take the Negro race to a new and better plateau, one that would get us pretty close to the same playing field as Whites. Oh, no, this could never happen! And Heaven forbid if any Whites joined the cause! But they did. Out of all the crimes that were occurring in the United States at this time, Hoover put them on the back burner and spent so much of his time trying to take the Panthers down. If any of you are interested, watch the powerful documentary on the Black Panther Party at https://fmovies.taxi/film/the-black-panthers-vanguard-of-the-revolution.qonj/o48p54.

The Black Panthers wanted only good things for the people of their community. They strived for decent housing, better employment, the means for a *true* education and not one that put empty holes in our history, a fair and balanced judicial system (Hah!), and freedom from white oppression (double Hah!). The BPP created free clinics and a breakfast program for children in black communities, who often went to school on an empty stomach. The Panthers were also knee deep in "Black is beautiful" and often elevated the black-man-black-woman relationship, mainly as a means for Blacks to come together, stay together, and work together toward a common goal. During this time, the BPP went so far as to demand all black men be exempt from fighting in the military. Remember what Seale and Newton said about Vietnam:

How can you have a black man going over there to fight a yellow man for the white man who stole his land from the red man?

These words are funny but so powerful at the same time. The FBI knew it and wanted to shut these leaders up. What better way to take down an entire community? Take out the leader(s). While the police were watching the BPP, the BPP was watching the police. Cops had to be monitored because they were one of the major causes of the violence occurring in black communities. Ice Cube's representation of the police was almost identical in the movie *Straight Outta Compton*. Now, the FBI told America that the Black Panthers were the greatest threat to the country, deeming the members to be nothing more than domestic terrorists. Theodore Kaczynski, the Unibomber, was a domestic terrorist; he killed and injured over a dozen people. Who did the Black Panthers kill?

After Nixon got into office, things grew even worse for the Panthers. The police were basically given the thumbs up to kill Panther members, starting shootouts the

BPP could never hope to win (Sounds like Tulsa all over again.) Nixon also gave Hoover free reign to dismantle the Panthers in any way he saw fit, which Hoover called "vigorous law enforcement." Now the police and the FBI had no reason to hold back. Hoover positioned black informants (aka traitors) within the organization, and these informants *helped* the Panthers acquire guns and then conveyed the information to the FBI. When law enforcement raided Panther headquarters, they went in with guns blazing. Making an arrest was the furthest thing from their mind.

Panther leader Bobby Seale was still alive but he was in jail. When he went to trial, he decided to represent himself. A white, racist judge refused to allow Seale to defend himself, and had him chained and gagged to keep him from speaking. Wow! At the same time outside the courthouse, a new voice of the Panthers, 20-year-old Fred Hampton, spoke on behalf of Seale. Hampton had an amazing speaking voice and people of *all* colors listened to him, especially when he said, "You can jail a revolutionary (Bobby Seale), but you can't jail a revolution!" Hampton had it in him to be the next "messiah" for the black race. He spoke in a manner similar to Martin Luther King and the FBI saw him as dangerous. We all know what happened to King, and it is interesting that Hampton realized he would not die of natural causes or in some kind of accident. Police raided Hampton's apartment while he and most of the occupants were asleep. What occurred next, law enforcement officials called a shootout, yet only one bullet from a Panther member's gun was ever recovered. Sounds like premeditated murder to me. Police used sub-machine guns and riddled Hampton's body with bullets. When they saw that Hampton was still breathing, though barely, they started shooting again. Another raid on the Panthers occurred during the day in front of hundreds of witnesses, including the media, which was, in effect, responsible for preventing the police from committing outright murder once again.

One of Hoover's last stratagems was to pit Panther leaders Eldridge Cleaver and Huey Newton against one another. He was extremely successful in his efforts. Because of the deaths and imprisonment of some of the Panther members, as well as the overwhelming pressure from our wonderful government, the BPP eventually died down. Although there were others who attempted to resurrect the Black Panther movement, it was never the same.

If there ever was a *super-super predator*, Hoover personified the role flawlessly. If there really is a Hell, I hope this man has napalm in his panties...*every day*!

EXPERIMENTS CONDUCTED ON THE BLACK MAN

As you can see, this wonderful government and country of ours has committed some of the most heinous and barbaric crimes against Blacks; and Hillary had the audacity to call *us* super predators. But one of the lowest and dirtiest maneuvers our government has ever done is experiment on black men with the syphilis virus. Using Hillary's own words, "...without *conscience* and without empathy," our government, the number one *super predator*, decided Blacks were the best guinea pigs for studying the side effects of untreated syphilis. In reality, this was just another one of their schemes to eradicate the black race. Our government chose men from Alabama who were mostly sharecroppers who could barely read or write. Whites did not even think about choosing more educated Blacks for their experiment. Many of these men jumped at the chance to enroll in this *clinical study*, once the word FREE was mentioned (remember...free isn't always good). These men got free food, free *healthcare*, and some type of life insurance policy. The experiment, called the *Tuskegee Study of Untreated Syphilis in the Negro Male*, started in 1932 and lasted until 1972, even though penicillin had been discovered to kill the syphilis virus by *1947*! Yep. That's right. The cure was purposely kept from these men so the *study* could continue. Before 1947 ended, many of the men had contracted blindness and others had died. The government was very much aware that syphilis was contagious; consequently, these men infected their wives and girlfriends, and sometimes passed it on to their children, making the experiment an effective means for eradicating a portion of the black race.

This so-called *study* was supposed to last for less than a year; but even after black university officials and medical staff saw it continue past the deadline, they said nothing. Some were afraid to tell their black brothers the truth because of fear of retaliation from the government or loss of their prestigious position at the school. Regardless, someone should have told these men what was really going on. This is another reason why I say black people do not work *together* toward a common goal, at least not enough. I guess our government was having so much fun playing God with black people's lives, the study just had to continue.

This reminds me of the story of Henrietta Lacks who died in the early 50's from cervical cancer. Doctors took her cells, also known as HeLa cells, without her or her family's consent and used them in medical research. Lack's cells were mass produced and used all over the world; they helped build a multimillion-dollar industry that manufactures and sells human biological matter. We know who was behind this and you can bet Lack's family never saw one penny of the profits.

This is no different from how doctors and hospitals keep the foreskin from a circumcised male infant. The foreskin is a hot commodity in the field of medical research because of its healing capability. If grown properly in a lab, one tiny little foreskin holds an abundance of genetic matter that can develop into the length of a football field. This is over a hundred yards of new skin! Why am I telling you this? I'm about to let you know.

Collecting a baby's foreskin has also developed into a multi, million dollar business. The foreskin is used for many medical procedures, such as skin grafting and insulin development. Think about all the diabetics in the world today and then think about all the money parents could have made. Oh, yes. As a parent, you have the right to keep your baby's foreskin and sell it. Have any of you ever had a doctor explain this to you? Of course not. Not to me either. They are not going to tell you because they want to keep the money for themselves. So, think about your children excelling in science and then becoming scientists with their own lab. Do you see where I'm going with this? This is one of the reasons I always push for education. Again, people, this is a million dollar industry and with all the babies many black females are having, black scientists could possibly control a large portion of this market. Some low-income black families could even afford to send their kids to the best schools to keep this type of cycle going.

Now, there's no telling how long the Tuskegee experiment would have gone on if someone had not blown the whistle. This was the *only* reason the study ended and led to a human rights lawsuit that eventually forced the government to pay out $9 million to the remaining survivors. This was one of the dumbest and most insane types of experimentation ever. Our government knew that untreated syphilis would produce the same effects in white men as in black men. C'mon now! The War on Drugs, the war on women, Hell, there's been a war on Blacks for…ever!

Mass amounts of Blacks affected with syphilis is almost unheard of today; now we have to deal with HIV and AIDS. Blacks have the highest rate of HIV/AIDS in this country, and it has been like this for quite some time. Years ago, fingers pointed at Africa as being the origin of the disease, and many people (white people) actually believed this. Racist Whites spread rumors that African men contracted the disease from having sex with monkeys; but much of the public was ignorant to the fact that the United States *produced* and *patented* the AIDS virus. Oh, you'd best believe the government cannot deny this; and if our government can experiment with syphilis, then why not with AIDS?

AUTISM

The Tuskegee experiment conducted by our white government was definitely horrendous, but there may still be a tragedy occurring in this country today: the uncanny rise of autism in black children, especially boys. Before the year 2000, the overall autism rate in the United States was about 1 in 175, and 1 in 125 during 2002. As 2006 rolled around, the rate increased to 1 in 110. Years later, the rate spiked to 1 in 88 and is now at an unprecedented rate of 1 in 59; in some states, the rate is worse. Both black and Latino children outnumber white children with autism in many regions of the country. Are you interested in why the rate is so high? You should be. The reason I bring this to your attention is because of all the horrible actions our government has taken against black people over the years. Call it a conspiracy theory if you want; but again, if the United States government can conduct a syphilis experiment on black men, then who's to say it would not do the same on black boys?

There are a few experts, and I mean only a few, who believe that autism has a deep connection to childhood vaccinations. Having our children inoculated to prevent certain diseases is a necessity, but we need to challenge doctors on the *amount* of shots our children receive in just one visit. I know of a mother who refused to let the nurses give her child three vaccinations during the same visit. What do we really know about the side effects of these vaccinations, especially if so many are given at one time to a small child whose immune system is not as strong as an adult's? As a parent, you have the right to tell doctors that you want to space these shots further apart.

WHAT ABOUT AFRICA?

White, European *super predators* did the same to Africans. They used experimental vaccines on African citizens without their consent, which resulted in the death of too many to count. Trump may view countries in Africa as *shithole* regions, but gold and diamonds, which Whites covet and will do anything to obtain, also come from this *shithole* land. Many of us—- Black or White—-fail to remember that *every* fruit and vegetable originated from this *shithole* land, even rice. How 'bout it? I bet Trump didn't know that. You can also bet that he doesn't know that Africa means "The Mother of all Mankind."

A SECOND CHANCE
FOR DUI OFFENDERS

In much the same way as racist Whites (AKA super predators) of the early 20th century did not want to see Blacks prosper in any way, there are still a good number of them today who feel the same. They do not want to see us sitting behind a bench in a court of law. They want us on the other side, pleading out our case and owing the city thousands of dollars, or better yet—-locked up. How about getting your driver's license revoked? Most of us are aware that black drivers get their license suspended or revoked almost five times more than Whites, even for the same type of driving offense. The only reason former Illinois Governor Rauner pushed for previous DUI offenders to get their license back is because this was a way for the state to generate more money (just my opinion). This is similar to Illinois and other states legalizing marijuana...to bring in more revenue. Do not believe for a second that he was trying to pass this bill strictly out of the goodness of his heart. Think about it. The price of a vehicle sticker in Illinois is around $150. Multiply this by a measly 10,000 drivers (approximately *one-third* of DUI offenders in Illinois) and Illinois will receive about $1,500,000. And we cannot forget about the cost of the written and driving tests they will most likely have to take after all this time, as well as the "breath ignition interlock device" that will have to be installed in their vehicle. If Governor Pritzker moves on this bill, where do you think all this extra money is going to go? I have no idea; but this new bill is a complete one-eighty from the way things usually happen. Some conspiracy theorists believe Rauner may have made a deal with some of the insurance companies to insure high-risk drivers, in return for a cut of the profits. The premiums and deductibles will probably cost an arm and a leg. It's not as if deals like this have never been made before because how many Illinois governors have gone to or are in prison? Again, it's all about the money.

BILL CLINTON
AND OUR PRISON SYSTEM

If our government cared about us, do you think it would have ever gone along with former President Bill Clinton in implementing the *Three Strikes, You're Out* bill? This is a bill in which black men suffer from the most. Am I right or wrong? I'm not referring to hardcore killers, rapists, and pedophiles who deserve to spend the rest of their life in prison. I'm talking about our husbands, sons, and brothers put away for life for offenses that are petty compared to the ones I just mentioned. To me, this is just another form of population control; but instead of having their life taken away, black men are taken away for life.

This is also a perfect means for our government to utilize free labor. Why should our *caring* government pay wages for work done to federal highways, buildings, and bridges when it has hundreds of thousands of prisoners at its disposal? This is one of the reasons why our nation built more prisons; it was not because of the overcrowding issue. When Clinton and his administration created this bill, the idea of *expanding* free labor was already on the table. Black people, listen up! The 13th Amendment has a loophole that permits modern day slavery to exist in this country in the form of "punishment for crimes." The idea of free labor is an incentive for our government to lock people up and lobby for longer prison sentences. The prison system in this country is a billion dollar industry and companies such as IBM, Boeing, Motorola, Micro-soft, AT&T Wireless, Texas Instrument, Dell, Compaq, Honeywell, Hewlett-Packard, Nortel, Lucent Technologies, 3Com, Intel, Northern Telecom, TWA, Nordstrom, Revlon, Macy's, Pierre Cardin, and Target have capitalized on this free labor. This is only a few of them. Even Bob Barker from the *Price is Right* found a way to make millions from the prison system.

Now, do you honestly believe Bill Clinton would have drafted a bill so unfor-giving if the majority of people (statistically speaking) in prison were White? Hell no! If that were the case, he would have called the bill *45 Strikes and You're Out*.

PRISON STATISTICS

Blacks make up roughly 12-13% of this nation's population, yet they make up approximately 35% of the prison population, and that's just the national average. Although the United States makes up only 5% of the world's population, it has 25% of the prison population on the entire planet! Wow. No other country in the world can compare to the United States, when it comes to locking up its own people! In states such as Maryland, Blacks make up almost 75% of the prison population, yet the state is only 30% Black. The reason I am speaking on this is because so many white people get numerous second chances and there is a noticeable discrepancy between the two races, in terms of sentencing.

Let me touch on the subject of driving offenses one more time. It is common knowledge that anyone can look up a person's criminal record through a city's court website. Check out particular white individuals with DUI offenses and compare it to those of Blacks. I have come across black offenders with one or two DUIs who have lost their license. A while ago, someone tipped me off to a white man who has 13 DUIs! OMG! And this cretin is still driving...with a valid license! Unbelievable! I guess he knows somebody who knows somebody who knows somebody.

Crap like this is not supposed to happen but it does. Our justice system is screwed up, and we all know it. It's ridiculous and it pisses me off! What pisses me off even more is Trump wanting to give major drug dealers the death penalty. Is he for real? Last time I checked, using drugs was a voluntary action.

Can we say the same for rape? How many women go out and get raped on purpose? And answer me this. How in the world can a drug dealer get more prison time than a pedophile or rapist? Anyway, if this ever becomes law, 30% of doctors and half the CIA will be on death row. How 'bout it?

NAFTA

If our government cared about us, it never would have gone along with President Bill Clinton's other project. The Trade Bill (NAFTA), which did away with many previous import restrictions. This led to big U.S. businesses moving overseas, taking hundreds of thousands of jobs away from hard working Americans. Why do you think Detroit ended up in such a sad condition? The jobs disappeared and the cities dried up because we were (and still are) relying more on importing goods than creating them in this country. I hate to admit it, but Trump and I are on the same page with this one. A lot of older people can remember when over 80% of products used in America were manufactured right here in the United States. By 1980, this percentage dropped to approximately 70%. I came across a website that said experts now claim that at least 65% of all products are made here in the United States. I find this extremely difficult to believe since nearly 100% of clothes and shoes in my closet are imported from other countries, mainly China. Don't believe me? Check the labels. In fact, check the labels on everything in your house and see if you can find *five* items MADE IN AMERICA. Good luck.

THE CLINTONS

As the years went by, more jobs disappeared overseas. It really cracked me up to hear black people call Bill Clinton "our first black president." Why? Because he had a cool voice and played the saxophone? Or could it be because he *got some* on the side with that Monica chick? Could this be why so many black men could relate to him? Sorry; linking black men to infidelity is a low blow, but I'm just so mad at how delusional black people can actually be.

How much money do you think was involved with this trade deal? A deal that screwed up the livelihood of many black, middle-class families, as well as hardworking Americans in general. Black people are so delusional! I'm going to say it again. Wake up! Bill Clinton never did anything worthwhile for black people and you definitely could never look to Hillary for help. She was without a doubt involved in the trade deal. Both she and Bill got paid and continue to get paid! Plain and simple. With the impending impeachment process that was looming over his head, what happened? A war. Or was it? It sure was mighty convenient that a war erupted across the ocean the same time Clinton was facing possible impeachment. There is a good chance that this war was fabricated only to take the focus off him. If so, it worked marvelously. If any of you ever watched the Michael Moore documentary on this subject, then you know what I'm talking about. This seems strangely familiar to what went on with our current president. Trump was too slow to respond to the disaster in Puerto Rico after Hurricane Maria; and most of us know that it was because people of color live in Puerto Rico. It's also because Puerto Rico has no significant resources our government can profit from. If white people had inhabited this same country, our government's response would have been immediate.

Trump was also criticized for calling NFL players "bastards" because of their protesting. Around the same time, the FBI and other agencies were investigating him for possible ties to Russia. What happens next? A mass shooting in Las Vegas in which 59 people died. Now, I am not saying the Trump administration had anything to do with this; but again, it sure was one hell of a timely coincidence. There are still so many unanswered questions about the shooter. The first is how did he get all those guns up to the 32nd floor without detection; and the second is why weren't the security cameras recording on this particular night? This is the Mandalay Bay we're talking about. It has almost 40 floors and over 3,000 rooms. I do not know of a single casino of this stature that does not have state-of-the-art surveillance. Several weeks later, the footage suddenly appears. Days and weeks before this tragedy occurred, the media's attention was on Trump; but once again, the public's focus was easily diverted. Hmm.

MORE ON BILL CLINTON

Furthermore, President Obama put Bill Clinton in charge of the relief effort for Haiti after the devastating earthquake in 2010. As secretary of state, Hillary was at the helm of this project. More than $100 million was on the line and was to be spent on long-term endeavors for Haiti. Now, just how much of that money do you think Haiti actually saw? Some experts say less than 4%. Hmm. Four percent of $100 million is roughly $4 million.

News sources from around the world were curious about how the Clintons managed to *choose* a construction company for Haiti's rebuilding when the project was supposed to go to the lowest bidder. It turns out (as far as I know) this particular construction company is, or was, affiliated with Warren Buffet, billionaire and contributor to the Clinton Foundation. Do you see how the pieces fit together? Whenever money is involved, you'd best believe the "little people" suffer first and they suffer the worst. How 'bout it? The Clintons got richer and did not get into a lick of trouble. Wow! It's always about the money.

This reminds me of the relief efforts for the Ethiopian famine during the mid-80's, which inspired Michael Jackson's *We are the World* video. Again, millions of dollars came up missing. The Ethiopian government, as well as other governments around the world, wanted us to believe that rebels stole a good portion of the donations to fund their militant organization. This could be true, but one thing bothered me. How did they get their hands on the money in the first place? It's not as if they simply waltzed right in and took it. A bunch of currency was not just lying on top of a kitchen table ready for the taking. How did these so-called rebels get the money?

All of these facts about the Clintons are common knowledge, but because some of you *refuse* to educate yourselves, you believed these people were God's gift to Blacks. Don't make me say it again! Bill Clinton did not help us to better our circumstances, and Hillary was not going to be of any use either. The only area she has always been good in is encouraging people to go out and vote.

ACCOMPLISHMENTS
OF OUR ANCESTORS

Look, even though Obama has left office, you should not feel sad. We should have never looked to him to better our circumstances anyway. Opportunities in this country exist for us, but they are not going to just fall out of the sky or into our lap. The task of finding them is entirely up to us! Look at the many accomplishments our ancestors were able to perform during slavery, as well as after slavery ended, all without the help of the government. One of my favorites, Sgt. Henry Johnson, a WWI hero who fought off German soldiers—- *after* they shot him multiple times. Johnson saved a fellow soldier from capture, along with his entire regiment; but because of our racist government, he received no medal of honor. It was France that awarded Johnson with one of the highest Medals of Honor any soldier could receive, the Croix de Guerre. Henry Johnson was only 5'4". Wow.

James Armistead (Lafayette) was a double spy for America *while* he was a slave. He was extremely instrumental in helping to win the revolution against the British in the 18th century. This was definitely left out of the history books.

Although Wentworth Cheswell was labeled as a white man, mainly because of his pale, light skin, he had at least 25% African blood flowing through his veins. He was the first known black man to be a judge. This was quite a feat since slavery was still going on at the time. Cheswell happened to have ridden with Paul Revere to warn people of the British invasion; he went one way, and Revere went the other. Whites left this bit of history out of our education, too.

How about Robert Brown Elliott who, although born in England, came to this country shortly after slavery ended and became the first black man elected into Congress. Elliott used his authority in Congress to combat the Ku Klux Klan.

For those of you who do not know, it was a black man, Daniel Hale Williams, who, in 1893, performed the first open heart surgery... successfully.

Another black man, Charles Drew, created plasma blood transfusion.

In 1939, Jane Matilda Bolin became the first black female judge in the United States.

George Washington Carver created about a hundred products using the peanut, including shaving cream and cooking oil. By the way, Carver is said to have been castrated by his owner in his early childhood. The owner wanted to make sure no sexual encounters occurred between his daughter and Carver because the two spent so much time together.

Can you believe Benjamin Banneker wrote an almanac? He was mostly self-taught, and became a mathematician and astronomer. Banneker wanted to change his life and he did.

TIPS TO CHANGE ONE'S LIFE

Many people view success as either being rich or famous, or both. This is not necessarily true, at least not in my book. A successful life entails having a good and loving family, being able to provide for them, giving them everything they need, not everything they want, and having enough money to sustain yourself during old age. If you do not currently possess any of these assets, then maybe it's time to try something else. If you want your life to change—-then change it. There's no one stopping you but you. Remember, no matter how horrible you think your life is, no matter how dire your circumstances are or used to be, life is what you make it.

I am encouraging all of you to start making new choices and change your life, if this is what you want to do. Work together and finish what our ancestors tried to do. Create a positive goal for your family and try to carry on where the Black Panthers left off. I do not claim to be some major activist and I'm not advising you to start an organization. I am just saying more of us need to promote the black race as much as possible and in a positive manner. The Black Lives Matter movement is a fantastic start, but it is only a small part of the solution. Maybe we can start by eliminating the word N****r from our vocabulary. This is a slave word that was designed to be offensive, and does not promote black people in *any* way, shape, or form—-not even if you change the spelling. How 'bout it? I promote my black race, mainly through my job in TRIO. I encourage *all* students from *all* walks of life, but I'm not ashamed to say that I focus more on black students. I do this out of necessity, not preference.

The first bit of encouragement I am offering you is to get off welfare as soon as you are able. It's a trap. Too many of us are dependent on the government for, let's say, our survival. Do not mistake what I am trying to say; there is absolutely *nothing* wrong with receiving government benefits, and there is no reason to ever be ashamed. Everyone needs a little help from time to time. According to the U.S. Department of Agriculture, "approximately 22 million households receive SNAP benefits, 40% whites, 25% blacks, and 13% Latinos." Of course, many white Americans will want to refute these figures only because they make up approximately 67% of the country's population, compared to Blacks who make up only 12%. But is it okay that Blacks have lower paying jobs, often receive inadequate education, and deal with unemployment at a much higher rate than Whites? Well, maybe this balances things out a little. Don't view receiving state benefits as an insult to your intellect or your character. For me, these benefits were a stepping-stone. What I do believe is that turning government handouts into a career is an outright insult to our ancestors.

THE LONG LINE OF DEPENDENCY
AND COMPLACENCY

For those of you who have forgotten, our ancestors were *forced* to depend on white slave owners for their survival; after all, Whites had all the power. Dr. Carter Woodson, author of "The Mis—Education of the Negro," had some very powerful words to say about dependency:

History shows that it does not matter who is in power... those who have not learned to do for themselves and have to depend solely on others (the government) *never* obtain any more rights and privileges in the end than they did in the beginning. (How 'bout it?)

This dependency was not something slaves wanted, nor found pride in. Remember, we are descendants of not only Mandingo warriors, but also kings and queens. In all actuality, white slave owners depended greatly on slaves for their own survival. Think about it. Slaves cooked the food. Slaves cultivated the fields and picked the cotton. Slaves tended to the livestock. However, this type of dependency was not the same because slave owners could always buy another N****r.

It was not as if slaves could just easily take off and find a better job, a better home, or make a better life for themselves by going to college. At the time, their lives did not include words such as *decide* or *want*. What they wanted did not matter. Their choice in every aspect of life was taken away—-what they ate, what they wore, where they slept, and with who. This is 2020 and for Blacks, these two little words are spoken more than ten times a day. "I want the T-bone, medium well, with a stuffed baked potato, extra cheese." "I've decided to take the day off." "I want that black dress over there." Our choices are limitless. If our ancestors saw us today, they would probably think we were kings and queens...albeit foolish kings and queens.

When I mentioned that some black people today are insulting our ancestors, I was referring to the fact that many of us are in a predicament, similar to slaves. It saddens me to come across Blacks who can barely read or write, when our ancestors had to educate themselves in secret. If discovered, they faced the auction block, tortuous punishment, and, of course, death. As slaves, they had no public school to go to five days a week. They did most of their learning after working 14 grueling hours in the field, under the relentless heat of the sun. Our ancestors would no doubt roll over in their grave to see how many of us have squandered our chance at a good education, or at a chance to better our lives and the lives of our children. Many of us are far too complacent with what meager things we have and where we are in life, especially because of all the freebies our government provides. It is nothing but complacency and dependency that strangle the potential of so many Blacks.

All of us are aware that white slave owners provided their slaves with the basics: food, clothing, housing, and sometimes a little money, as well as medical care, if slaves did not doctor themselves. What is our government providing for those of you who are collecting state benefits? Food, housing, sometimes a little money, and medical care. The money, of course, can be used to purchase clothing. So, can any of us be called a slave today? Hell, yeah! Our situation is not that much different from slavery 150 years ago; we are just in a different type of slavery, a deception, a con. The main difference is that for our ancestors, slavery was a way of life. For Blacks today, 21st century slavery is a choice. As a result, many of us have fallen for it and can't get out... or don't want to get out. Who wouldn't like free food, free medical care, and pay a measly $64 a month in rent? The government knows this and takes advantage of our complacency and dependency. Listen up, people! Stop being delusional! This is the underlay for the overplay! It's the government's way of holding black people down. It's bad enough when we hold ourselves down. All these benefits are *gifts* from the government designed to distract us from evolving and progressing in society. Think about it.

In the 60's, a surge of black people attended college; some of them even went to all white colleges, especially after Jim Crow laws started to dissolve. How do you think certain Whites felt about this? Well, during these same years, our illustrious government decided to expand welfare programs, creating, or so it thought, the War on Poverty. Lyndon B. Johnson, the president at the time, spearheaded this initiative. His goal was to "break the cycle of poverty," and make "taxpayers out of tax eaters." Johnson alleged that his new program "would bring an end to the conditions that breed despair and violence," those being "ignorance, discrimination, slums, poverty, disease, and not enough jobs" (dtn.org). One question: Is this what happened? Far from it. Too many Blacks fell for this line of crap, and ignorance, discrimination, slums (ghettos), poverty, disease, and unemployment not only continued, but flourished. The stability of the black family truly began to crumble at this time.

The longer we keep accepting *freebies* from the government (not including financial aid for college), the longer we remain in the same stagnate position. This is why so many of us sustain poverty mentality *for life*. The more Blacks who remain dependent on the government means fewer Blacks will be in middle-class neighborhoods, in the middle-class income bracket, earn a better than average living, or be in positions of authority. Stop asking what the government can do for you; instead, ask *yourself* what you can do…*for you*.

Now, make no mistake; I would love to pay less than $100 in rent, but I refuse to accept the deplorable living conditions that often come with it. Slaves *had* to endure horrible living conditions; we don't. Don't ever forget that. We have a choice! What's funny about this is that over the years, I've heard black people say "They (the government) owe me!" Why? Because you're Black? Come on now! If you did not experience the horrific tragedy that occurred in towns such as Harrison, Arkansas, in the early 20th century (as a means for ethnic cleansing of the black race), then the government owes you nothing! If you are not a recently freed slave and over the age of 155, then the government does not owe you a damn thing! The majority of people the government does owe are dead and buried…or living on a reservation. Do not try to get a free ride for something that happened to your great-great-great granddaddy.

Now, I consider myself lucky to have a mother who would not *settle* for anything just because of a low price. After our father ran out on us (Wow! That's a new one), it was up to her to put food on the table for her four girls. We ended up on welfare, but she did not move us into a dangerous neighborhood, nor were any of us forced to share our breakfast with rats or roaches. Stop settling, people! If you continue to settle, it is very likely that your children will grow up and do the same. Again, slaves *had* to settle; we don't! How 'bout it?

There is nothing wrong with wanting more if you're willing to work hard for it, and not take it from someone else. My mother worked hard but she constantly looked for a better job. When she finally landed a job at Kraft, she soon left welfare behind and bought a house. So, if any of you want a better life, work for it! Plain and Simple. Most of the higher paying jobs require a college degree but many are worth it. If you do not want to go to college for four years or more, try truck driving. This is an industry that is never going to go out of business and is always looking for new employees. Distribution companies are so desperate for drivers that employers are hiring 80-year-old seniors straight out of retirement. Most new drivers start out at $40,000 a year, directly after training school, which usually lasts for six to eight weeks. How much are you making right now?

WELFARE AS
A LIFE-LONG CAREER

Now, let's continue on with turning welfare into a career. I'm sure some of you know exactly what I'm talking about. *Some* women have a system when it comes to having babies, strategically spacing them apart, so they never lose their state benefits until they are nearly 60 years of age. They really do this! If I'm lying, I'm dying! First, let me tell you about "Cassandra." I did not know Cassandra very well; we just happened to live in the same apartment building. I lived on the second floor and my living room window faced the front of the building. One day, Cassandra and a friend were sitting on the front steps chatting. Cassandra mentioned to her friend how fast the years were flying by and that she could not believe her son (her only child) was getting ready to turn 17. The friend asked why it was such a big deal and Cassandra replied, "Because in less than two years, I'm going to lose my benefits." The friend asked Cassandra what she was going to do and Cassandra replied, "Whatcha think I'm gonna do? I'm gonna have another baby." Wow! What a reason to have a baby. Maybe it's this desire to be so dependent on the government that causes some women to think like this.

Now, let me tell you about "Vera." I knew Vera from over 35 years ago; we went to the same high school. By our senior year, She already had two children by two different guys and was receiving state benefits. As expected, Vera followed in her mother's footsteps in every way. At the time, Vera had seven brothers and sisters; two of them were still in grade school, and her 40-something-year-old mother was on welfare. It was very close to graduation and many of us were discussing our future plans while riding the MTD bus to school. It was one of those what-are-you-going-to-do-when-you-get-out-of-school days. When the question was put to Vera, she replied, "I'm gonna keep having babies. God made our bodies (we women) to birth babies and that's exactly what I'm gonna do." Vera was true to her word. She gave birth to about seven children and remained on welfare throughout her adult life (a perfect example of poverty mentality). I saw her from time to time over the years, mostly in grocery stores. Since we had been in the same grade in high school, I knew how old she was. I had just turned 42 when I spotted Vera in Meijer. (The store was having a killer meat sale.) She was several feet away from me, but I knew it was her. Her back was toward me; and when she turned around, I not only recognized her but her bulging belly as well. At 42-years-old, Vera looked like she was ready to bring baby number eight into the world, giving the two young children next to her a new brother or sister.

I couldn't help it. Two things immediately popped into my head. One: She could have at least put some lotion on her crusty feet. And two: Hand-cut booty shorts don't look good on a pregnant woman *with* crusty feet. What this boils down to is that at the age of 42, Vera will continue to receive state benefits until she is about 61-years-old, the day her unborn child turns 19. If the retirement age does not change, she will be eligible for partial, social security benefits approximately 3-4 years later, and receive full benefits five years after that. Wow! Vera is in her mid 50's now, and if it were not for menopause, she'd probably be on baby number 12. A word to the wise for any of you who are following this same tactic. It's going to come back and bite you on the ass, because how you live in the present will reflect how you live in the future. If this is not clear enough for you, let me say it another way. If you are poor and have absolutely nothing right now, you will most likely be poor and have absolutely nothing when you're a senior citizen. How 'bout it?

WHAT SETTLING CAN GET YOU

O f course, how much one receives in state benefits depends on how much money one earns each week. I know several women who receive nearly the maximum in benefits because they make sure to work only part time. I'm going to use "Letty" as a perfect example. Letty has four children ranging in age six to sixteen. She never works more than 25 hours a week and usually makes no more than $8.50 an hour. This amounts to a little over $10,000 a year before taxes. But Letty does not always work the entire year. It's her habit to sometimes work only six months out of the year; some years she doesn't work at all. Come tax season, she claims two of her children, getting an average refund of $6,000-$8,000. She "sells" the other two children to friends and splits the refund 50-50, 60-40; I don't know. Add all this money together and Letty actually brings in some healthy stacks each year. Not bad, hey? In fact, she often makes more money from her tax refund than she did from her job.

One of the downsides to this system is Letty being a *settler*. She and her children practically lived in squalor, much like our slave ancestors did. She lived in one of the worst neighborhoods in Champaign, Illinois, exposed her children to crime, filth and stray bullets, and forced them to share their meals with the live-in vermin…and there were a lot of them! The roaches were so at home that they had their favorite TV show! Letty had all this tax-free money, but what did she choose to do with it? Nothing that would truly benefit her and her children. Oftentimes, her refund was gone in less than a month. But

Letty made sure that she always had money for liquor, cigarettes, her choice of drug, and some of the most expensive clothing that the average person could not afford. Letty also carried around an authentic Gucci handbag and drove a newer-model Chevy Tahoe. If she was able to obtain these particular items, why couldn't she provide adequate housing for her children? By the way, Letty's kids slept on dinghy mattresses on the floor. But hey, she sure looked good driving down the highway!

SOCIAL SECURITY

The more money a welfare recipient earns, the lower the limit is for Link benefits. The more children a welfare recipient has, the higher the limit is for Link benefits. These are two reasons why *some* females work only part-time and have more children than they can take care of without government assistance. How this benefits them in the present will certainly not benefit them in the future. My, oh, my. That sounded so good I have to say it again. *How this benefits you in the present will certainly not benefit you in the future!* It's difficult to believe, but I have actually come across females who proudly boast about the government "taking care of them for life." For life? Are you kidding me? Let me say it again. Black people are so delusional.

Who cares if Letty and other females are making thousands of dollars under the table. Just answer one question. Where will this get them once they are in their 60's? Not very far. After earning less than $10,000 a year for nearly 45 years, they will most likely find themselves back to depending on the government for their survival. During retirement age, most seniors will be travelling, visiting relatives, and enjoying their grandchildren. Without adequate retirement benefits from one's previous place of employment, many seniors have to rely totally on social security. Remember when I said, "The more money a welfare recipient earns, the lower the limit is for Link benefits?" Almost the same concept is involved with the social security program. The more money Americans earn in their lifetime, the more money they receive from social security, up to a certain limit. Not so with individuals such as Letty. Let me break it down to you.

According to the Social Security Administration, if Letty continues to work 25 hours a week and does not earn more than $9 an hour, by the time she retires in 2030 (at the age of 66), she can expect to receive about $850 a month. This amount does not reflect an increase in future prices. Do you honestly think $850 a month is enough to live on? Not for people who have to pay rent or mortgage. Not for people who use gas or electricity. And not for people who want to eat. If we calculate an increase in future prices, then there is a chance Letty will receive around $650 a month. This paltry amount could have tripled or quadrupled if Letty had worked more, instead of being so dependent on the government all of her life. Letty is drowning in poverty mentality. Think about it...$650 a month. What could any of us possibly afford with this measly amount? Furthermore, since I seriously doubt Letty can eat and pay her rent and utilities at the same time, she had better see if Wal-Mart is still hiring greeters in 2030. And inform her grown kids that mommy needs a place to stay...forever.

TAKING CARE OF BUSINESS

Putting needs *before* wants is something responsible adults do nearly every day of their life, regardless of race or color. I have relatives, and I'm sure you do, too, who are never without their recreational *needs;* and you know what *needs* I'm referring to. These relatives work full or part-time, yet somehow, they are short on rent money at least once or twice a year. What's up with that? Then there's that proverbial phone call many of us get from a particular relative we sometimes strive so hard to avoid. We know exactly what's going to be said: Hey, my power got shut off. Can I borrow $50? $100? Borrow? Like we'll ever see that money again.

Some distant relatives of mine got their water shut off for almost an entire month and, of course, all seven of them continued to use their one and only toilet each day. They had to constantly add water to the toilet and force it to go down the pipes. Where they got this water from, I don't know. Sometimes they would scoop out the urine and feces with a bucket and dump it in trash bags, or bury the crap in their backyard. Even though the stench in that house was between a dead skunk and a decaying body, they never once stopped smoking, drinking, or drugging. Wow! You can't blame this one on white people.

These are the same types of individuals who go through all of their children to keep the utilities on. Parents who use their children to get the utilities turned on are irresponsible individuals. Somehow, they are able to get credit cards in their children's name, too. Those of you who do this crap obviously don't care how this will affect your children once they reach adulthood. Think about it. You, the parent, are the cause of your children having bad credit, even before they are old enough to establish credit. This doesn't make a lick of sense; and you should be ashamed of yourselves! One of the first things out of the mouth of some of these women is "I'm a grown-ass woman." Well, act like it! Grown-ups—-responsible grown-ups—-handle their business! How 'bout it? I have heard of only one case in which a child grew up and sued her mother. Before going to court, this female could not understand why her credit was so bad. When she discovered that her own mother was the cause, she did not just sit back and take it; she fought back, and won. Can anyone say "FRAUD?"

We cannot forget about the relatives who never, *ever* have a backup plan. Both my husband and I have relatives who love to travel, but they never take enough money with them when they leave town. Well, they do take enough money; they just spend it all. Over the years, my husband has received calls from one or two family members, which start out like this: "I'm stranded and I need some money to get back home." Now, these individuals went to where-everland with hundreds of dollars, if not thousands; but somehow they found themselves broke, and without the means to get back home. We knew exactly what they had done with all that money. Once, they had the nerve to ask for money to buy a plane ticket. Are you kidding me? My husband *bought* them a bus ticket, and didn't even think about sending them any money. One of my cousins had $600 on her Link card one night, and $20 dollars left on it by the next morning...all without bringing home a single bag of food. Wow.

FUNERAL EXPENSES

Now, some black people have the audacity to *demand* from their relatives a particular type of funeral when it's their time to leave this earth… as well as the design of the casket. How the hell are you going to lay out the rules for your own funeral when you neglected to *ever* purchase life insurance?! In other words, you have no money! You're going out the cheapest way possible…cremation! During your lifetime, if you have been nothing but a burden to your family, financially or otherwise, do not be one in death! It's not right and it's not fair. If you do not have life insurance (a necessity many low-income blacks are lacking), then you better not die! It cost money to die; it costs money for burial and cremation; and too many of us take for granted that our loved ones will pay for everything. If you keep on this way, the bottom of your obituary in the newspaper will say *Donations accepted at ———- Church*. PEOPLE! LISTEN UP! If you do not have the money for your own funeral, then you do NOT get to dictate the terms! Besides, you won't know anyway.

BECOMING A BURDEN

When I talk about being a burden, I am referring to individuals—-especially adult males—-who lay up in their parents' house and do absolutely nothing! You know the ones I'm talking about, the ones who sleep until noon and bring their friends over at all hours of the night, get high, make a mess, and eat up all the food. I'm talking about the ones who measure their manhood by how many children they have fathered, yet fail to be a dad to any of them. I'm talking about the ones who refuse to work because they do not want child support taken out of their paycheck. I'm talking about the ones who sell drugs out of their momma's house, instead of getting a job or an education.

Now, if you do *not* want to be a burden to your family, *especially* your mother, then get off your ass and help. If you are not working, keep the house clean, cook dinner; do something that will take the strain off your mother. I happen to know a 50-something-year-old man who does not work, collects disability checks (although nothing is physically wrong with him), still lives at home with his mother, and has her washing his dirty clothes. How long is crap like this going to continue? Granted, some of the fault belongs to the mothers who allow such behavior in their home, but this is still ridiculous! Get up! Get a job; or get out!

EDUCATION

I know finding a job can be very difficult for many black people, especially ex-felons. Some of you men may have to perform duties that you feel do not reflect your manhood; but compared to not working at all, the best you can do is suck it up until you find a better one. After all, a man's gotta do what a man's gotta do. Right? Since I work at a community college, I come across people from all walks of life, including ex-felons. A particular student, who was also an ex-felon, majored in auto mechanics. He maintained a 3.2 GPA (on a 4.0 scale), graduated, and landed a job at a major car dealership. Right after he was released from prison, he had to make a decision (as so many ex-felons do) between settling back into his old life and risk being locked up again, or finding a new lease on life. His friends made sure to let him know he was more than welcome to start selling drugs for them again, but he chose not to. Good for him.

College is a way for many of us to have a better life, sometimes much better than the life of our parents and ancestors. Have you forgotten how slaves were intentionally kept ignorant, so they could never find themselves on the same intellectual level as their white masters? During slavery, Whites possessed all the knowledge (in terms of reading and writing) and did whatever was necessary to keep it out of the hands of Blacks. This was because they knew that knowledge is power; and if any slaves got hold of this power, Whites would lose total control over them.

Over 150 years ago, Whites severely punished slaves for seeking an education. Today, way too many Blacks do not even attempt to further their education, something our government readily pays for! What's it going to hurt to give college a chance? What's the worst that could happen? A degree and a better paying job, perhaps? Or maybe you're just afraid of failing. Please! The only thing you should be afraid of… is failing to try at all. How 'bout it?

EDUCATION FOR BLACKS
BEFORE 1970

When our government finally created public schools for Blacks in this country, they were quite different from white public schools. Most of the schools black children attended in the late 40's and 50's were run down, especially in the South; and the curriculum was far below average. It was *purposely* designed to ensure their intellect remained inferior. My mother told me that when she was a sophomore in an Alabama high school, she had the same books white kids had used in the sixth and seventh grade. Wow. For many whites, nothing was worse than an intelligent N*****. This brings me to another sad issue. I always make it a habit to promote getting a college education to young black individuals. Of course, I get replies such as "College ain't for me." "It's too hard." "I don't want to spend four to six years of my life going to school." Then I ask them, "What are you doing now?" and "Where do you see yourself five years from now?" Silence. I actually had a young man say to me that college is for white people. And the answer I hate the most is "I'm not smart enough for college." Wow! If this is not being down on one's self, I don't know what is. Black people are so delusional! We are *all* intelligent and we are *just* as intelligent as Whites are; but how we use our intelligence is what matters the most! But maybe this young man has a point. Although he could tell me in

.04 seconds how many grams make up an ounce, he couldn't tell me how many feet are in a yard. Sad.

If college is not for you, try a trade school, such as construction or truck driving, as I mentioned earlier. If you do not want an education, the least you can do is get more involved in your children's education. Do NOT leave it up to the teachers to educate your children because many of them will be left behind, especially in overcrowded public schools! The average teacher will never have enough time to help 20 plus students on a one-on-one basis. Do you think our government cares? If our government cared, a *gajillion* public schools would not have shut down all across the nation.

SCHOOL CLOSINGS

From 2012 to 2013, almost 1,500 public schools closed their doors. This fact is from the National Center for Education Statistics. Nearly 130 public schools closed in the Chicago area, and Detroit is not far behind with 126 closings. More schools closed in 2015. Dr. Umar Johnson, a black activist, historian, lecturer, and author, emphatically states that charter schools may replace public schools in the very near future. If this occurs, Johnson believes there is a chance charter schools may evolve into private institutions. Who's to say this will actually happen? But what if it does? This means that parents may end up paying a hefty tuition for their children. No more $50, $75 or $100 paid at the start of the school year. I'm talking about thousands of dollars *each* year for *each* child. Are you ready for this type of expense? If you're not, then you'd better start thinking about home schooling or scaling back on the number of children you plan to have. The bigger question here is what happens to our children if we cannot afford to pay their school tuition. Hmm. The majority of people believe this will never happen, but it is still something to think about it.

MORE ON EDUCATION

Because of the way national matters are changing so rapidly in this country, parents should already be a big part of their children's education. We parents need to take the initiative to educate our children *outside* of the classroom because they are not learning enough in school, especially about their black heritage! Public libraries are at our disposal and the internet is just a click away. Each semester at my job, I come across students who are barely literate. How in the world did they make it through high school? You already know the answer. School officials passed them through because of their age. They might also have been part of the problem many public schools in this nation face each year: low SAT or ACT scores. For some reason, many individuals in our government believe that schools with higher SAT scores should receive more funds. At least this was Bush Jr.'s way of thinking. Which schools have higher SAT scores? The ones in middle or upper income neighborhoods. So, the lower the test scores are for certain public schools, the lower the amount of federal funding the school district receives; at least, in some cases.

On the other hand, public schools receive thousands of dollars per student if the student has an IEP, an Individualized Education Plan. The government established this mainly for children with some type of learning disability. Now, this is all good and dandy but the problem stems from many school professionals over-diagnosing kids just to get additional federal funding. At my job, I come across several students with an IEP. Do I think every one of them should have it? Absolutely not. I'm not an expert or a psychologist, but I can tell the difference between students who need extra help and those who just don't want to do the work. But I am curious as to why wealthy kids do not have as many IEPs as low-income kids. The problem could very well be environmental, as many sociologists suggest, but I still think it's all about the money.

Many of you parents out there may have a child with an IEP and a documented learning disability; but you have to wonder if your child really needs it, or if the school is just trying to get more money. IEPs do benefit students, but they benefit schools a lot more. Go back to the school and request to terminate your child's IEP, and I bet you will have a small fight on your hands. IEPs can also place a stigma on children, causing them to believe they are less intelligent than their peers. The feeling some children get from having an IEP is equivalent to the indignity they may feel from riding the "short" bus. Think about it.

Due to issues such as these, many of our black children, as well as most children in poverty, usually do not receive the same education as children in middle or upper-class neighborhoods. This has a lot to do with our socioeconomic status (SES), where we live, how we live, our level of intelligence, how involved we are with our children's education, and how much money we earn. And when it comes to Black history, a large amount of schools have taken this subject out of the curriculum. DACC went almost ten years without a Black History course, but the new college president approved of bringing the subject back just a couple of years ago. This is why we never knew about the smart black women who were portrayed in the movie *Hidden Figures*. Come on, people. Exercise your mind and the mind of your children! It's not difficult. Get into the habit of learning just one historical fact each month about our ancestors. You'll be amazed at what you find.

EDUCATION FOR BLACKS
BACK IN THE DAY

When I was growing up in the 70's, I learned about five famous black people in elementary school, excluding the ones who were on television at the time: Martin Luther King, Crispus Attucks, Rosa Parks, Harriet Tubman, and Thurgood Marshall. I did not think about it at the time, but when I got older, I told myself, "Those must have been the Blacks white people deemed appropriate for us to study." I had never heard of Nat Turner, the Black Panthers, or Malcolm X, not even from my mother. Why didn't our school curriculum include learning about Nat and Malcolm? Because they were too militant for white people. These men coveted the mentality of "You smite me, I'll smite you back." They were not the type of men who would readily turn the other cheek; they were not peaceful like Dr. King was. They had no reason to be because Whites weren't peaceful.

It was the same with Native American history. I grew up believing Native Americans were blood-thirsty, scalp-stealing savages. The Westerns during this era did not aid in my perception of their character. Years later, I discovered Whites were the actual savages, the *super predators*, who slaughtered hundreds of thousands of Natives, slaughtered the buffalo to decimate tribes, and stole their land for *white expansion*, as well as for the gold that was on it. Not only that, I came across some academic articles which stated that white men invented scalping, at least European Whites during Medieval times. Maybe the natives were just returning the favor.

This reminds me of the book "Lies My Teacher Told Me" by James W. Loewen. It was a straight-out lie that Christopher Columbus discovered America. First of all, how can someone claim to discover a region that is already inhabited by thousands of Native Americans and Moors (Don't know what a Moor is, look it up)? I call what Columbus did an accidental visit. Furthermore, America was not the region Columbus was searching for in the first place; it was the West Indies. This is why he called the natives *Indians*. Our textbooks, as well as the teachers, neglected to tell us that Columbus was cruel; he murdered many natives in cold blood and enslaved others, just as he did when he arrived in the Bahamas. On top of that, he and his crew infected many natives with an STD. So, today we have a national holiday for a man who enslaved and murdered innocent people, got lost, and accidentally arrived in America. Wow.

It was the TV miniseries *Roots* that helped open my eyes to the real injustice our ancestors endured. As a young girl, my eyes teared up when I watched some of the scenes, in particular, the ones where white slave owners tore families apart. It was not until my mid-20's when I learned about black cowboys. I loved watching westerns as a kid, so I was thrilled to hear that Blacks were busting broncos and going on trail drives with the best of them.

LOST AND FORGOTTEN HER-ITAGE

I discovered that a black, female Jazz singer was the real face behind Betty Boop. White people changed her race.

Bessie Coleman, being Black and a female, could not reach her dream of becoming a pilot in America; so she became one in France.

Many of you might not know that there were countless books banned in the 60's and 70's, because they provided the true account of the atrocities Whites did to Blacks, as well as American Natives. Our white government wanted to keep its *own* race ignorant to their *super predator* ways.

When European Whites went to Egypt and saw the African features of the Sphinx (Oh, boy!), they used it for target practice until the wide nostrils disappeared and the thick lips became thin. Wow!

Why did whites bend over backwards to keep so much of our heritage from us? They did not want us to know or to be proud of the great people of our own race. They wanted black children to believe that in order to be some-one, they have to be white; and because they wanted to ensure white America remained under the illusion that they were superior to us. This is no different from believing that Jesus, who had "hair of wool" and was born in Jerusalem, located on the continent of Africa and inhabited by *dark-skinned* people, was actually a white man—-the *only* white man with blond hair and blue eyes—-in all of Africa. C'mon now! The proof of Jesus's race was in the hands of Whites at one time, yet they chose to bury it. Do you actually think they want the entire white race to know they have been praying to a man of color for centuries? The KKK would throw the biggest tantrum in history and other Whites would have heart attacks. There would be more suicides among the white race than there were after the 1929 stock market crash. How 'bout it? The more I read, the more knowledge I acquired. Once I got older, nothing could keep me from learning more about my black history.

Poverty has always been a major issue in black history and some people actually believe that Blacks created poverty for themselves. Untrue. I don't care what anyone says. Check your history, people; the government, and wealthy Whites who ran the country, *created* poverty for Blacks since the day our chained ancestors stepped foot on American soil! To this day, they continue to be successful in the perpetuation of poverty for Blacks, but only because we *allow* it to continue! How 'bout that?

THE TRUTH ABOUT THE
WILLIE LYNCH LETTER

A few years back, I came across an article called the "Willie Lynch letter: The Making of a Slave." Man, did this article capture my attention! In the letter, it tells slave owners how to keep their N*****s in line for 300 years. Wow. Now, even though I know a black man from the 1970's, Dr. Kwabena Ashanti, I believe, is the real author of this article, it was still mind-blowing to read. Near the beginning, "distrust, envy, and fear" are mentioned. The article explains how to get slaves to distrust one another by introducing fear and envy. The endgame is to make slaves trust only the master (the white man). Hmm. Now 300 years have come and gone, but I can see this concept still happening today. For example, my husband, who is a mechanic, has his expertise questioned by black people on a daily basis. After he tells customers what's wrong with their vehicle, some of them turn to the white guy he works with for confirmation. This sort of thing happens all the time, Blacks believing Whites are more intelligent. The guy my husband works with sometimes calls one of his *white* mechanic friends for advice, instead of asking my husband, who is ten feet away. On more than one occasion, my husband diagnosed a problem for this same co-worker but instead of giving my husband his props, he took *all* the credit.

Now, I'm not gonna lie; there are a bunch of black people I do not trust, including some of my relatives. Distrust is what has kept black people from coming together and merging into one powerful entity, something Dr. King, the Black Panthers, Malcolm X, and even Johnnie Cochran wanted. This envy stems from more than just "what they got;" it also includes the rivalry between dark-skinned Blacks with coarse hair, and light-skinned Blacks with "good" hair. (Please watch the short video called "Black Doll, White Doll." located at the end of the *Willie Lynch Letter*.) This envy is still going on today, even among 6 and 7-year-old little girls. C'mon, people; we have never had the option of picking and choosing our parents. We have no control over this; but we all see this division between the "shades" in every aspect of life: television, magazines, video dancers, sports wives, celebrity wives, even places of employment. As parents, we need to be vigilant in ensuring that our dark-skinned children, especially girls, never develop an inferiority complex about their skin color. The Lynch letter says, "Distrust is stronger than trust and envy stronger than adulation, respect, or admiration." What do you think?

The article also touches on "breaking the Nigger." There is one particular way to make this successful: First break the mother. How did they accomplish this?

"Take the meanest and most restless nigger, strip him of his clothes in front of the remaining male niggers, the female, and the nigger infant; tar and feather him; tie each leg to a different horse faced in opposite directions; set him afire, and beat both horses to pull him apart in front of the remaining niggers."

Whites are not resorting to this method of killing today, but they (cops) are still murdering black men in front of our eyes. This is partially why many black mothers whooped their children so severely back in the day. This method was handed down generation to generation to prevent children from angering *the white man*, and possibly losing their life to him. Remember, I said *one* of the reasons.

Now, this system for breaking the negra female has another intended outcome:

By her being left alone, unprotected, with the MALE IMAGE DE-STROYED, the ordeal caused her to move from her psychologically dependent state to a frozen, independent state. In this frozen, psychological state of independence, she will raise her MALE and female offspring in reversed roles. For FEAR of the young male's life, she will psychologically train him to be MENTALLY WEAK and DEPENDENT, but PHYSICALLY STRONG. Because she has become psychologically independent, she will train her FE-MALE offsprings to be psychologically independent. What have you got?

You've got the nigger WOMAN OUT FRONT AND THE nigger MAN
BEHIND AND SCARED...by throwing the nigger female savage into a
frozen psychological state of independence, by killing the *protective male image*,
and by creating a submissive dependent mind of the nigger male slave, we have
created an orbiting cycle that turns on its own axis... *forever*...

Wow. The dismantling of the male image as protector has lasted for a long
time, and is still in destruction mode today. These words remind me of how
many single women lead black households. I grew up in one, but I always
wished I had a father in my life. My mother had to move "out front" and become "psychologically independent" because my father was an alcoholic with
a gambling problem. He was MENTALLY WEAK and DEPENDENT on a
drug. He even pawned some of our possessions to pay for his addictions. My
mom stepped up to the plate and took care of her business.

The Lynch letter tells slave owners that this method will cause black males
to grow up to be cowards. This has worked to some extent. Now, before you
go off half-cocked, let me explain what I'm talking about. A black man is not
afraid to confront another man who represents some type of challenge or
threat. A black man is not afraid to protect himself or his loved ones. By no
means is a black man a coward in this context. But—-it seems to me that some
black men are afraid of evolving, perhaps even progressing. The type of progress I am referring to does not have anything to do with keeping up with the
latest smartphone, or investing in holographic technology that will eventually
become standard issue in households across the globe. I'm talking about internal progress, the kind of progress that takes intelligence, motivation, de-
termination, and hard work, the kind of progress that also facilitates these
attributes. Stealing, selling your body, or selling drugs has absolutely no connection with internal progress. These things are easy to do, and I know several
people who follow one or all of these professions to make a living. Why? It's
not cool to be smart? It's not cool to wear pants without your underwear showing? If you move out of the projects or the hood, does this make you a sellout?
Now, there is no way I can forget to show the Lynch phrase "It is necessary
that your slaves trust and depend on us." Hmm. How many of us are still de-
pending on the white man (the government) today?

This dependency some Blacks have on government handouts has a direct
correlation to our attitude toward poverty. If living in poverty does not faze

you, then don't read this section. Everyone else...read on. If you are in poverty right now and spend a large portion of your weekly paycheck partying (drinking and drugging), then you are likely going to stay in poverty for years to come. If you make less than $15,000 a year (single, no dependents), yet you walk around in Gucci, Armani, and something from Kanye West's clothing line, then poverty is perfect for you. If you have been receiving state benefits for more than 25 years straight, you'll probably receive them for 25 more. And if your vehicle looks better and is cleaner than your own home, then you and poverty go together like two peas in a pod. How 'bout it?

ASIAN OWNED
BEAUTY SUPPLY STORES

There is something else that aids in the continuation of poverty for many low-income Blacks: Beautification. Now, I know we all want to look our best when we go to work or hit the clubs, but the amount of money some black females spend on weaves and extensions is mind blowing. I was working with a student one day; and since we were on good terms, I decided to ask her how much money she spends on her hair and nails each month. She said that $70 went toward her nails and approximately $250 went toward packaged hair. This price did not include the cost of putting the weave in, which can be $150, or as much as $200. Wow. Now, this may not seem a lot to women who are earning a decent wage, but for those who are working part-time and making around $10,000 a year, this puts a huge dent in their pocket. On an annual scale, some of you spend over $3,000 a year, more than this for others. I used to get my nails done twice a month and I hated spending the money. So, I went to a store and bought everything I needed to do my own nails, as well as my own hair. The money I save now goes toward shoes and clothes, items that last a lot longer than store-bought hair. Remember, I'm not knocking you, just trying to save you some money.

In 2014, Asians, mainly Koreans, owned roughly 10,000 beauty supply stores in the U.S. I have no idea what the number is today, but get this: Black women in this country buy close to 10 times more hair care products than any other race; yet only 1% of us owns a beauty supply store! I knew two black women who operated their own beauty store. Where are they now? Out of business because people of their own race shoplifted and broke into the stores. What was taken? Hair. What does this mean? It means that Koreans are making billions of dollars from black people's thirst for *better* hair. We cannot get mad at them because they found a way to make a better living here in America than in their own country. If I had a product that Koreans desperately wanted, I'd market it and have a chain of stores around the country…maybe some in their country, too. The kicker is that many Koreans dislike and distrust Blacks more than White people do! At least, this is the impression many of us have. So, if any of you are aware of Black-owned beauty shops, support the owners. I do, and will continue to do so as long as the owner stays in business.

FINAL THOUGHTS

Think of life as a deck of cards. Whatever hand you're dealt, you have to decide whether to hold them or fold them. Though you may not always get the hand you want, there's no do overs. If you fold them, you're just giving up. If you hold them, then you have to make a play. Since it's *your* life, you have to decide what that play will be. I often wonder how the status of black people could have turned out differently, if our ancestors had made a different play. How would our lives be today? We will never know.

People, a great many of us spend too much energy fighting among ourselves, trying to get over on the government, delving deep into criminal activities, jumping from one female to the next or from one guy to the next, and doing absolutely nothing positive. And if you do not have anything positive to say to your children, if you do not encourage and motivate them on to bigger and better things, then find someone who will! It is unbelievable how some black mothers encourage their seven and 8-year-old daughters to dance like strippers, yet they won't encourage them to read a book. I went to a birthday party for a young child, and when she started dancing, I thought the only thing she was missing was a pole. What we should be doing is spending our energy on expelling all the negatives in our life. This includes people. Remember the words of Biz Markie: I can do bad by myself. I don't need no help to starve to death.

We also spend too much energy killing each other, which is 1000 times worse than cops killing us. I remember back in the day when real men were real men. When guys had a dispute of some kind, they duked it out with their fists until a winner was declared. After that, the dispute was squashed. They did not run home, whining like a little baby and come back with a gun, like a coward. Yes, I said coward. It is cowardly to spray bullets from a vehicle when there are innocent people around. It is cowardly to shoot into a home and not care if a child gets caught in the crossfire. Just recently, a 3-year-old toddler was shot in the chest; he died—all because a bunch of cowards had to bring their dispute around people who were not even involved. Again, if you are the man you claim to be, then find a way to settle these disputes without putting innocent bystanders in harm's way. This is what real men do. They take the fight far, far away. How 'bout it?

Unfortunately, for many of us, growing up with a decent and loving father was just not in the cards. As I said earlier, my dad ran out on us. He popped into our lives every few years or so; but after a while, the thrill was gone. I no longer thought of him as my father because he became a stranger to me. One year, he showed up—-out of the blue—-at my sister's job. Yes, she was shocked to see him, but even more shocking was the T-shirt he was wearing. My sister looked at the shirt, which read, "The World's #1 Dad," and asked him why he was wearing it. He replied, "Since none of my kids ever bought me one, I had to buy it myself." If that had been me, I would have asked him, "Do I have any half brothers or sisters I don't know about?" If so, maybe he was a good father to them, but he sure wasn't one to us. If any of you parents ever have to buy a T-shirt that elevates your status as a parent, and your own child did not buy it, then that child is trying to tell you something.

Regardless of the circumstances in your life, do not waste time blaming the father who ran out on you. Pity him, instead. Some of us miss out on having a loving and decent mother as well. Do not blame her if she got strung out on drugs and allowed the state to take you away. Pity her, too. They both missed out on something beautiful...you. Stop blaming them for where they put you. Blame *yourself* for staying there! Whatever happened in the past cannot be changed. Listen; in this day and age, it doesn't matter where you come from. What's important is where you're going and what you're going to do when you get there. So, if you want to have a little more in life, stop trying to keep up with the Kardashians, especially if you do not have the Kardashian's money!

On second thought, scratch that! Go ahead! Keep receiving those disability checks when there's absolutely nothing wrong with you. It's no big deal that you won't have enough income to live comfortably in your old age.

Keep throwing your money away on Armani and Gucci when you know damn well you can't afford it.

Keep spending hundreds of dollars each month on manicures and pedicures, and fake hair.

Keep putting thousands of dollars into your tricked-up vehicle while you're still living in subsidized housing overrun by roaches.

Ignore the fact that it would benefit you to use any extra money as a down payment for a house; unless, of course, you think riding around with $4,000 rims on a $500 car is more important.

And above all, remain dependent on the government and keep accepting that free food and free housing for the rest of your life. Just make sure you never forget to say, "Thank ya, Massuh!"

THE END

www.ingramcontent.com/pod-product-compliance
Lightning Source LLC
Chambersburg PA
CBHW070535290526
45790CB00002B/507